Spiritual
Direction
and the *Metamorphosis of*
Church

Brenda K. Buckwell

Spiritual Direction and the Metamorphosis of Church

The General Board of Higher Education and Ministry leads and serves The United Methodist Church in the recruitment, preparation, nurture, education, and support of Christian leaders—lay and clergy—for the work of making disciples of Jesus Christ for the transformation of the world. Its vision is that a new generation of Christian leaders will commit boldly to Jesus Christ and be characterized by intellectual excellence, moral integrity, spiritual courage, and holiness of heart and life. The General Board of Higher Education and Ministry of The United Methodist Church serves as an advocate for the intellectual life of the church. The Board's mission embodies the Wesleyan tradition of commitment to the education of laypersons and ordained persons by providing access to higher education for all persons.

Wesley's Foundery Books is named for the abandoned foundery that early followers of John Wesley transformed, which later became the cradle of London's Methodist movement.

CONTENTS

Appendices

FIGURES AND TABLE

Acknowledgments

The grace of God, the love and breath of the Holy Spirit with the ever-living presence of the risen Jesus is the catalyst behind, before, within, and through this book. I am humbled by God's presence, which anoints my life and has brought me thus far. Without God, the vision, creative energy, and Divine spark of endurance, the ministry of Living Streams Flowing Water would not exist. Hence neither would this book. Together we celebrate God.

> *Loving, generous, and gracious God, thank you for the gift of words. Especially, thank you for your precious Word of life. I dedicate this book to you, Jesus. May your transfiguring Word lead in the process of becoming new through the metamorphosis of spiritual direction. May both author and reader be drawn closer to your heart. Grant us your power, presence, and creative transfiguring energy. Through being formed into greater Christlikeness, may we become your people of love in community. Amen.*

Thank you to my friend and mentor, Dr. Dwight Judy. With his insight, encouragement, and support, I have learned so much. Thank you to my spiritual director and peer supervisor, who companion me along the way. Thank you to the many students who have tested and refined all the concepts of this book through semesters of prayer and engagement. Thank you to the numerous congregations that shaped, in part, my inward formation for practical ministry. A special thank you to CenterQuest, The Rueben Job Institute for Spiritual Formation at Garrett Evangelical Seminary, Ashland Seminary students, and the Louisiana Area of The United Methodist Church for the testimonies of God's transfiguring presence through spiritual direction training. I am indebted with gratitude for the ministry specialists whose wisdom is highlighted within. It is with sincere gratitude that I give appreciation to Kylee Baumle, the author of *The Monarch: Saving Our Most-Loved Butterfly*, and

St. Lynn's Press, who grant permission to use the extraordinary facts from her book. Thank you, Kylee. I join with you in great love of monarch butterflies.

The foundation of this book is from my doctoral dissertation through Garrett-Evangelical Theological Seminary Evanston, Illinois, titled *Rediscovering the Contemplative Tradition: The Formation of Protestant Clergy as Spiritual Directors Within the Twenty-First Century.* Unless indicated otherwise, all quotations from ministry specialists and past participants are from the research of the Louisiana Conference United Methodist Church's Academy, then Academy of Spiritual Formation. This Academy is no longer in existence. I am greatly appreciative to Rev. Dwight Judy, professor emeritus at Garrett-Evangelical Seminary, and Rev. Carole Cotton-Winn, former director of the Louisiana program, and retired Bishop William Hutchinson.

Finally, thank you to my children, grandchildren, and family, who are my delight of life and for whom I strive to be *Amma.* They are God's gift of practical love, forgiveness, and ever-deepening faith. Thank you for your constant prayer and encouraging support, without which I could never have crossed the chasms in life and experienced the depths of unleashed formation.

A NOTE FROM THE AUTHOR

This book has taken years to write. The topic and importance of transfiguration is at the heart and soul of my life-desire. For me, this *is* the gift of spiritual formation. It is the lifelong pursuit and practice of spiritual disciplines,
particularly spiritual direction, that open the way for God's inner light to
literally create our lives anew. The magnitude of my passion for this spiritually forming process is at times almost overwhelming to my spirit. That is
probably one reason why this book has taken years to write. Another is that
God has formed me through the years. I have soaked in God's presence as
learner, practitioner, and leader. It is my hope that these words may in some
small way anoint your life and ministry.

This transfiguring process is best depicted for me through the divinely
inspired creation of the monarch butterfly. When I learned that God formed
the caterpillar with the innate, awe-inspiring possibility to morph into a
butterfly, my heart was smitten. The question of how we as church leaders
and congregations could experience this new-life process of metamorphosis has occupied my mind and heart for years. I use the term *church* in an
inclusive sense. Church is wherever you find yourself leading others toward
deepened awareness of God. This could be in a congregation, campus ministry, small group, fellowship gathering, camp, seminary, or even your own
family. Church is wherever you share God's presence. For simplicity's sake, I
interchange "church" and "congregation" for all Christian gatherings.

I use the term *transfiguration* rather than *transformation* to depict the
interior illumination of God-shaping energy within humanity. To transform could possibly be an exterior-only change, from one way of looking or behaving to another. We get "transfigured" from the Greek word
Μεταμόρφωσης, which literally means "metamorphosis."[1] Transfiguration
highlights the interior shift in heart as God's presence shines forth from the

---

1   *The New Interpreter's Bible*. 1995. Volume 8. Nashville, TN: Abingdon Press. Page 363.

center of our being to our exterior actions, words, and mannerisms. Spiritual maturation and formation occur as we potentially become translucent so that God's glory radiates from within and through our lives and the congregation. This formational movement toward God's heart and greater union with God is depicted within this book as a downward spiral. As the church descends the spiral of this illuminating metamorphic process, it potentially becomes translucent with God's glory illumining our lives.

Through the metamorphic life stages of the monarch from a caterpillar, to a chrysalis, and finally to a butterfly that takes flight, we will ponder how spiritual direction has the potential to awaken the church and its leaders to new depths of illuminating God-love. Beginning with the ravenous hunger of the caterpillar, we discover our own deep restlessness and inner hunger for more than is currently experienced. Do you have an inner hunger? Are you restless? St. Augustine of Hippo stated, "Thou hast made us for Thyself, O Lord, and our heart is restless until it finds its rest in Thee."[2]

This book is for all who desire new possibilities for opening self and community to God-sized potential. Whether you are a pastor, scholar, church leader, judicatory official, or seeker of faith, this book will provide a pathway of discovery through the tools of spiritual direction training. We move first to spirit-formed leaders and then to training the heart of the congregation. Ultimately, we awaken personal leadership with potential as God illumines our lives and communities.

As the leader descends the metamorphic molting process of stepping out of old ways into new life, he or she can then share spiritual direction tools with the congregation. This two-step process of leader and congregation has the potential to become one pathway toward spiritual awakening. Through the three stages of awakening, we discover that now is the opportune time for taking flight in ever-deepening faith formation. The final sections of this book provide testimonies to the power of a transfigured life through spiritual direction. The afterword provides resources for leaders and congregations.

God's creative Word is powerful and brings about new life. Through my own process of becoming, I have come to the realization that now is the time for my passion to take flight into the cultural chaos of the church, society, and within our personal lives. May it be so for you as well.

---

2   This quote is from St. Augustine of Hippo, found at https://www.goodreads .com/quotes/42572-thou-hast-made-us-for-thyself-o-lord-and-our. Accessed June 17, 2019.

THE LAYOUT OF THIS BOOK

The metamorphic process of spiritual formation, and the primary tools from spiritual direction training, are shrouded in mystery. Using words to describe the powerful and creative presence of God's Word transfiguring human life causes us to plumb the depths of our wisdom, feelings, intellect, and vocabulary. Spiritual direction assists the directee, that is, the one coming for spiritual direction to access greater articulation of the mysterious movement of God within. With increased ability to articulate God's inward formation comes the wider potential to influence others with God's luminous light. This book begins with the basics of spiritual formation. What is Christian spiritual formation? How are spiritual direction and the tools from spiritual direction training foundational to all ministry? Recognizing the overarching umbrella of spiritual formation ministry, we can turn our focus to the metamorphosis of awakening that moves along the Möbius strip from leader to congregation.

Spiritual Direction and the Metamorphosis of Church is divided into six major sections. At the end of each section is a Spiritual Direction Readiness Assessment and Congregational Examen. This examen aids the reader in discerning leadership and congregational availability to God's transfiguring light and illuminates personal life and church culture. There are no correct or incorrect responses to the Spiritual Direction Readiness Assessment and Congregational Examen. Only you will know how you respond. God will meet you right where you are and lead you into what is possible.

Following the sixth section, an afterword provides suggested overarching implementation of spiritual directors' training tools. Thoughts to gain a new life perspective with tools from spiritual direction training and online resources for teachers, pastors, judicatory personnel, and congregational leadership give substance to the afterword. It also includes a list of training resources for spiritual direction. Following the afterword are appendices that provide in-depth instruction for specific prayer tools, if you would like to know more.

The individual reader of this book might ask the following questions: Why is this the opportune time within the church and the culture at large to awaken a new potential through spiritual direction training tools? How ready, willing, and available as a personal leader am I to experience spiritual direction? The following might be a question to pose to a congregation or may arise from within a congregation: Are we ready as a community of believers to move beyond the way it has been, to soar to new heights through our luminous God's transfiguring love, with the tools of spiritual direction training? Both the individual and the community are invited to consider how spiritual direction could become a possible pathway for the metamorphosis of church.

The journey to new life is often murky and difficult. It may be tainted with resistance from within and beyond the self. One way to approach potentially difficult or new topics that stretch our faith beyond current experience is through creativity. Throughout this book, there are frequent quotes leading us through the transfiguring process of metamorphosis from caterpillar to butterfly. I hope you enjoy the illustrative word pictures of the monarch's life journey as your imagination expands and spreads new wings for spiritual flight personally and as a congregation.

Following the introduction of the hunger within, section 1, "A Process for Life," begins with a tale of transfiguration, which provides an imagined experience of a monarch caterpillar changing into a butterfly during the process of metamorphosis. From the beginning of its life, the caterpillar repeatedly experiences that its skin becomes constrictive. Hidden in God's womb, ripe with new life tools, the old way of living is loved into its greatest possibility. Themes from the caterpillar's metamorphosis are carried forward throughout this book.

An exploration of three-way listening ensues, making it known that trinitarian listening discloses God to be the true guide in spiritual direction. Through discovery of the biblical foundation for new birth and God's desire to communicate, create, and redeem, the gift of spiritual direction is born.

Section 2, "The Wild Wilderness," takes us into the wild wilderness of culture. From disorientation, chaos, and confusion to unleashing God's illuminating possibility, we discover foundational spiritual direction wisdom from the margins. In this section, we nourish the hunger within as an ever-expanding passion and ever-deepening faith for leaders is revealed. These Spirit-formed and Spirit-led leaders empower others on the formational journey of faith. Four historical influential leaders of faith introduce how the tools of spiritual direction training open the way for spiritual awakening. Highlighting these men and women leaves us to wonder if we too could become influential leaders who emit the luminous love of God lived in community through the tools of spiritual direction training.

The historical perspective of formational leadership begins with the *ammas* and *abbas*, the spiritual mothers and fathers of the third through sixth centuries. Then highlights for St. Benedict, St. Ignatius, and Rev. John Wesley complete the historical picture. This historical lens begs the question of how we could be living into the next great awakening. Why did these giants of faith-wisdom seek new ways for living faith and sharing God's presence? These noted historical figures were closely knit to a body of believers. As these leaders' spirits were ignited by the passionate love of God through God's spiritual guidance, their brilliance of faith could not be contained. This transfiguring faith potentially awakens communities to new ways of living. As the formational foundation of the leader expands, questions such as these are mined in section 2. What is a spiritual awakening, and how do awakenings come about? What does metamorphosis have to do with spiritual awakening?

Moving from the historic to contemporary church, we note similar stages of awakening. As we work through the disorientation and chaos of today's church, to truly morph from the old to new flight, intentionally Spirit-formed and Spirit-led leaders and parishioners are needed. Spiritual direction brings us collectively to the edge of God's new era in faith formation. The Third Way of Christ is embodied within humanity as we live transfigured lives manifesting God's light through the confusion of the world.

You, the reader, are invited to become a Spirit-led and Spirit-formed wisdom leader. Stages of faith will be explored, with an optional online assessment. As you gain even greater clarity about God's winsome faith within, the wonder of how you, a faith-wisdom leader, may influence a congregation looms before us, hence the dual focus of this book on leader and congregation. Section 2 begins with the leader, and section 3 focuses on the church.

The question for section 2's Spiritual Direction Readiness Assessment and Congregational Examen is from John Wesley. You will discern in what stage of awakening you are currently living. Further, an examen of which stage of awakening the congregation is being invited toward is explored. Are the leader and the congregation ready for the next steps of soul formation through spiritual direction toward greater Christlikeness? How intentional are you in expecting, anticipating, and discerning God's pathway?

In section 3, "Tools for Training the Heart," we move into practical and mystical aspects of training the heart. Together we discern teachable skills for self-knowledge, release of attachments and "rightness," how to become a non-anxious presence, action-reflection methodology, and the practice of holy listening and storytelling. These skills are formational for both leader and congregation. However, the focus of this section is on the congregation. As the threads of God's silence and nourishment are woven through this section, we discover that the spiritual disciplines center and anchor the soul of the congregation in new perspective.

In spiritual direction it is important to turn to wonder. Wonder encompasses the mystery of God in a broader scope than informational questions. It also removes the "rightness" and "wrongness" of response. After discussing each training tool from spiritual direction, there is a Pause and Ponder section to contemplate your experience of God's presence. The wonder to consider is how the soul of the congregation claims the prophetic edge of love in action within the harried, wild wilderness of our day.

Section 3 moves from historic one-on-one spiritual direction to a variety of expressions. Tools of spiritual direction have the potential to transfigure small groups from informational study groups to formational soul-shaping, silent-listening, love-in-action groups. As we move through this section, we will spiral toward the heart of God's formation through corporate spiritual direction for congregational wisdom and worship.

This lifelong adventure of spiritual direction is not for the faint of heart. Through each of these teachable skills and deepened experiences of God we may discover resistance from within and imposed by others. The gifts of storytelling and holy listening create sacred space for the community to receive the experiences of others. Like the molting caterpillar in need of new skin, it is easy to become stuck by limited beliefs, fears, doubts, and outside threats on our faith pilgrimage. Do the imagined cries of the caterpillar through the process of becoming a butterfly resound through our resistance? Is the process of becoming a new creation more difficult than first imagined? Are we tempted to fall back into known comfort? This third section concludes with a gentle look at these resistances and some possible ways of taking flight beyond the limiting leaps of life.

The Spiritual Direction Readiness Assessment and Congregational Examen provides an opportunity to ponder silence, self-knowledge, listening skills, and heart hospitality. You will examen how ready parishioners are to receive and see beyond outward presentation the living presence of Christ in others. Are there resistances limiting the leaps of your individual and collective inward and outward expression of Divine compassion and spiritual growth?

Inspiration comes to us through narrative in section 4, "Living Passion of the Awakened Heart," as stories of transformed lives are shared. Participants from spiritual direction training programs and classes tell their yearnings, hopes, and dreams from the Louisiana area training program, CenterQuest, and the seminaries. We will hear stories that address these questions: As one personally experiences the teachable skills of contemplative listening, what shifts within to open heart hospitality? How does spiritual direction training transgress the dividing lines of evangelical, traditional, and progressive? How does inward formation affect external action and mission of the church?

In section 5, "Reality, Possibility, or Pipe Dream?," we see that as God inspires and gifts us with courage, old habits of church potentially give way to God's new awakening. It is here that possibility is birthed as personal leadership is explored through the Leadership Diamond. It is this inner side of leadership that brings soulfulness to the transfigured heart of the congregation. Contemporary voices of ministry specialists resound with hope-filled testimony as the cry of the church is heard. We stand on the edge of God's new thing. Is it the opportune time for us to become midwives, helping to birth authentic community through deep soul-shaping?

The Spiritual Direction Readiness Assessment and Congregational Examen in section 5 offers an opportunity to ponder the gift of God's presence amid the current reality for leaders and congregations. As heart-yearning is revealed, the wonder of ethical implementation for individual, group, and corporate spiritual direction will be considered. The question for section 5 is, What is the heartbeat of your personal leadership?

Through the practices of section 6 we are set free for flight. With the amazing fourth-generational account of the monarch butterfly who stands on the foundation of what has gone before, we move from frenetic action to accessible tools that offer the potential to transfigure congregations. The imagination is sparked with Divine fire through contemporary spiritual disciplines to expand vision and become fertile soil for soul-shaping love in the community of church. The nuts and bolts of this section lead into the afterword to contemplate next steps.

The process of this book, much like the lifelong transfiguring process toward a Spirit-formed life, has been shaped through God's amazing guidance and birthed from the author's yearning heart. May the gift of these words open the way for your heart to hunger for God's new thing as you soak in the transfiguring process of spiritual direction and the metamorphosis of church.

INTRODUCTION
THE HUNGER WITHIN

The tears welled up in his eyes. Silently spilling over, they rolled gently down his cheeks. His eyes pleaded what his heart felt as piercing conviction.

> Is it too late? Why not earlier? Why didn't I learn on the inside of my heart this new way of listening, inviting others to deep listening of God's spirit?
>
> This is what has been missed in the church. I am guilty of it too. That is what I cry about. Why not earlier, why so late—is it too late? After thirty years of ministry, have I done any harm?[1]

What leads a pastor to this kind of heartfelt confession and lament? He was a good congregational pastor for thirty years. He taught the Bible to the people within the church. He preached a gospel that compelled people to believe. Yet, with a deep inward transfiguration of God's Word birthed into his life in new ways through spiritual direction training, he learned a deeper way of knowing. This deep, beyond-words knowing is reminiscent of the internal stirrings of God's presence knit secretly in the inward parts of our being (Ps 139:13–16). He wondered, "Why not earlier? Have I done harm?"

His heart hungered for a new way to live as Jesus loves. He lived the metamorphosis of expanding his awareness of God through spiritual direction training. Yet, his heart hungered. There was still so much more of God to experience. He sought to live this new understanding within the congregation, his family, and in all his relationships. He began years of seeking

---

1   Brenda Buckwell, 2007. *Rediscovering the Contemplative Tradition: The Formation of Protestant Clergy as Spiritual Directors within the Twenty-First Century.* A field research project report submitted to the faculty in partial fulfillment of requirements for the degree of Doctor of Ministry. Evanston, IL: Garrett-Evangelical Theological Seminary. Page 17. This quote and all quotes, unless otherwise indicated, come from my doctoral research with the Louisiana Conference of The United Methodist Church.

and reflecting on how he could best use the tools of spiritual direction in his leadership.

It is never too late. God's hunger stirs within, inviting us to the lifelong pursuit of being deeply heart-formed by God's energizing presence. The more we seek this Divine shaping of God in our inward nature, the deeper our hunger for knowing even more of God. The French Enlightenment philosopher Blaise Pascal spoke of this deep desire. Pascal stated, "There is a God-shaped emptiness within us that only God can fill."[2] It is this secret womb of God's hunger within that inspires our ravenous spirit to yearn for God.

For me? Hunger pains shot through my whole being. At first it was an indescribable feeling. A deep yearning burned within, drawing me further into the discovery. I hesitated to speak of it at the time. Thirty-plus years ago it seemed so personal. I wondered, *Who would understand this mysterious longing within my heart?* I prayed. I devoured books on the spiritual life. The written Word became my life preserver in the sea of everyday life and ministry. My heart burned as my foundational life Scripture unfolded before me.

The story in John 4 of the Samaritan woman's conversation with Jesus at the well captured my heart. Jesus sought her out. Jesus received her as she was. He did not condemn her. Jesus led the woman through spiritual direction to new insight. The result was a transfigured life. The concluding verses of this conversation speak the illumination of God's Word rising within her.

> The woman said to him, "I know that Messiah is coming" (who is called Christ). "When he comes, he will proclaim all things to us." Jesus said to her, "I am he, the one who is speaking to you." . . . Then the woman left her water jar and went back to the city. She said to the people, "Come and see a man who told me everything I have ever done! He cannot be the Messiah, can he?" They left the city and were on their way to him. (John 4:25–30)

---

2   *Wikiquote*, s.v. "Blaise Pascal," http://en.wikiquote.org/wiki/Blaise_Pascal (accessed June 7, 2007). Blaise Pascal was a French mathematician, physicist, and religious philosopher. His most influential theological writing was the *Pensées*, a "coherent examination of and defense of the Christian faith." Pascal was considered "one of the most important authors of the French Classical Period and is read today as one of the greatest masters of French prose. . . . The context of his work is best remembered for its strong opposition to the rationalism of René Descartes." *Wikipedia*, s.v. "Blaise Pascal," http://en.wikipedia.org/wiki/Blaise_Pascal (accessed June 7, 2007).

As this Scripture seeped deep into my soul, I began to realize the truth about the hunger within. Even with doubts, imperfections, and wonders, all humanity has the potential to become luminous vessels for transmitting God's Word and glory to others.

This text gives me great hope for our lifelong yearnings. We are a people with an innate hunger, just like the caterpillar. This lifelong hunger is ever-deepening as we grow in faith. However, unlike the caterpillar, leaves do not satisfy our hunger. Soulful listening to and embodying of God's Word is the process for the formation of our inward life and the satiating of our hungering spirit.

God has created this hunger within us. The innate desire to satisfy the hunger is there, if we do not dismiss it. Resistances rises. Fears of New Age mumbo jumbo stifle exploration of inward holiness. Cultural privatization of faith protests collective spiritual direction. However, for those that venture into the depth of God's love within, the potential for transfiguration of self and community abounds. As expansive Christlike character is formed within the individual, the Christian community can literally radiate love incarnate.

Are you ready to notice the hunger pains yearning deep within? Can you imagine the collective soul of the congregation hungering deeply beyond the bookend prayers of opening and closing meetings? Now is the time to awaken to our deepest hungers within as we seek to descend the spiral of formation toward union with God. Let us turn to the image of the caterpillar as we discover the wonders and imaginative process of metamorphosis within the womb of God satisfying the hungry heart.

One

A PROCESS FOR LIFE

The Egg Stage of Spiritual Life

The mystery of God is that God creates life that can transfigure from one form of life to another. The egg opens the potential for the caterpillar. The caterpillar morphs into the monarch. The wise female monarch listens deeply to the innate wisdom. She has firsthand experience of the ravenous hunger. She knows, beyond logical reason, that the tiny caterpillars spawned from her eggs will be hungry. Carefully, with great intention, she lays her egg on the milkweed plant, one egg per plant. She does not want to limit the life span of her offspring. She knows the competitive tendency of the newly born ravenous caterpillar to become cannibalistic.

Like the female monarch, we are invited to listen deeply to the indwelling of wisdom from God to satisfy our hunger. This is where the spiritual life begins. From the moment of our birth we have grace-given potential to be transfigured into God's great creation. This stage is more than our first conversion and profession of faith. We experience new beginnings continually throughout our lifetime of faith. These moments of new beginnings could be an enlarged perspective for living as Jesus' loves, a new way of praying, or an experience of God that causes us to reorient life. We are always beginners in faith.

> "The female lays her eggs singly; depending on the size of the
> milkweed plant, she will only lay one egg per plant. . . . The number
> of fertilized eggs a single female monarch lays varies greatly,
> determined by such factors as weather, availability of milkweed and
> her age, but it is probably somewhere between 400 and 500."
>
> Baumle, *The Monarch*, 20.

A Process for Life

How have or are you experiencing a time of new beginning in your spiritual life? What is it like for you? Who supports, mentors, and befriends you during this new experience of faith formation? The monarch caterpillar lays its eggs on the underside of the milkweed leaf. It is the safest place from predators, harsh rains, and wind. Where is your safe, sacred space?

Over the years, I have heard of similar deep hunger for God's formation. As I listened to the pastor speaking in the following quotation, my heart was in solidarity with him. The circumstances differ, but the sentiments and yearnings ring true.

> I had been invited to participate twice before. Each time looking at the invitation and tossing it in the wastebasket, thinking, *I don't need that. I am spiritual.* I thought I knew what faith and practices were about. Even when Katrina hit,[1] I felt I was doing a good job caring for myself and the congregation. . . . It was tiring work but rewarding. I was watching myself, pacing myself—or at least I thought I was. When I was asked if I could be given a break, I assured the asker, "No, that wasn't necessary." I was doing well; holding up under extreme conditions, or so I thought. . . . For the second time, another offered to give me a break. I declined. "This is what God has called to me." I wanted to be faithful. I was just certain I was watching out for myself and would be just fine as God cared for me.
>
> Then the time came, after months had passed, for me to visit my daughter who had been evacuated to another state. . . . It was quite a long drive, about ten hours. As I drove, I saw a flock of beautiful white birds. Watching them, I started to pray. That is when I

---

1   The mission field in Louisiana was the area devastated by Hurricane Katrina, 2010.

realized I hadn't prayed in a while, not for myself and my own journey. I prayed for the rest of the drive, all ten hours. When I arrived at
my daughter's, I realized instantly my own exhaustion. . . . there was
a deeper part within me that needed healed, needed fed—that
space where only God can touch. I hungered for that nourishment.[2]

As the realization of the depth of his hunger for God dawned, this pastor
diligently sought a sacred safe space to revive his weary soul. He responded
positively to the invitation of spiritual direction training. He knew he wanted
to find rest and God's potential healing. Pastors and congregational leaders
are faithfully dedicated to call and work endlessly through extremely stress-
ful and emotionally charged circumstances. Leaders may find themselves
spiritually and emotionally exhausted. Our hearts yearn to trust God even in
the midst of chaotic times. We know God to be faithful. Still, exhaustion and
deep hunger can consume our inward being and may catch us by surprise.

Through the process and training tools of spiritual direction, the leader
may open further to God's transfiguring illumination. This transfiguring
quality of becoming transparent so that God's light shines through our
lives is gained as we are progressively shaped into the image of Christ. This
inward shaping of divine energy, love, forgiveness, redemption, and constant presence of empowering Spirit can change our old habits into new
ways of being in the world.

Paul talks of this transforming process from old ways of thinking, seeing,
and doing to new perspective as we become a new creation in Christ. Paul
writes, "So, if anyone is in Christ, there is a new creation: everything old has
passed away; see, everything has become new!" (2 Cor 5:17). To illustrate this
newness, we now turn to the metamorphosis of the caterpillar turned butterfly to illustrate this morphic shift from one way of life to another.

A Tale of Transfiguration: From Caterpillar to New Life

As you read this tale of transfiguration, keep in the forefront of your heart
the wonders of how the metamorphic stages of caterpillar turned butterfly
can illustrate becoming a new creation. This potentially leads us all to weep,
"Why not earlier? Have I done harm?"

---

2   Buckwell, *Rediscovering the Contemplative Tradition*, 81.

The monarch butterfly is beauty floating upon the breath of life. My love of the black-veined wanderer led me to research its migration patterns. I marvel that such little wings, with great perseverance, could fly as far north as Canada and south to Mexico. The reality of this migration is that only the fourth generation of monarchs make the arduous flight. Each generation before opens the way for the opportune time of flight for the fourth generation. Since the life span of the previous generations is as short as ten days, all of this takes place within the northern hemisphere during the summer months. The migrating monarch lives much longer than the previous generations. But before it was set free in flight, it inched upon the earth.

Within a few short days, the monarch's life moves from an egg on a milkweed plant to a caterpillar. The life purpose of the caterpillar is to eat and gain strength for its morphing time. Faithfully, the caterpillar lives upon the earth, nibbling leaves and nourishing the potential within. From its earliest beginnings, the caterpillar has the greatest potential for freedom, flight, and new life. Two weeks following its birth, driven by innate forces deep within, the caterpillar spins its cocoonlike abode. The chrysalis is the mysterious womb where one form of life changes to another.

The descent into silent darkness looks to the outside observer as if all is lost. It appears to the human eye that nothing happens within the chrysalis. The way of life that the caterpillar knew comes to an end. The inward formation, known only in the mystery of God's silent womb, incarnates the caterpillar, transfiguring its life with potential, possibility, and perfection.

I wonder if it is a comfortable process to be shaped into a new form of life. What unseen hunger drives the caterpillar to enter the process of interior change? Does the caterpillar ever want to throw up its proverbial hands in defeat or scream that the difficult process of metamorphosis and transformation is much more than it ever bargained for? Does the caterpillar ever yell, "Not fair! I want to quit!"? Could the caterpillar ever beg, "Please, just let things go back to the way they were—the comfortable and known ways of life!"? Are there times of great stress, pressure, and unforeseen shifts in the caterpillar during this metamorphosis that seem more difficult than the caterpillar could imagine enduring? How painful is metamorphosis for the caterpillar? Is the caterpillar ever afraid of entering the unknown? Does resistance happen during the process of transformation? Could there ever be competing voices from within as life shifts drastically to become God's utmost potential and possibility? Despite all these possible questions, the caterpillar opens to the deep inner stirrings and consents to a life-shaping process. This process is dying to self, which gives way for new life.

At just the right moment, the life of the caterpillar is morphed into a butterfly. Still encased in the chrysalis, the butterfly waits. In stillness the butterfly hangs upside down, suspended as the mystery of God works. This is not a passive waiting. God's greatest beauty and potential is constantly and incrementally emerging as the Divine imprint of life becomes more and more a reality.

Inside that chrysalis, the light of God shines. Divine energy of presence and creativity unleash the fullest potential within the caterpillar as the butterfly emerges with new skill and character. No longer are the old habits of the caterpillar enough for life. In this state, awaiting timely Divine inspiration, the chrysalis becomes transparent for all to see God's beauty. This is the moment that transfiguration begins to illumine the exterior world. New life from within shines out for all to see. The butterfly is now ready to emerge with near perfection of freedom, flight, and formation. The butterfly takes up its mantle as co-creator with Divine Love. It expends energy to emerge from the limitation of the chrysalis. Life for the caterpillar is forever transfigured.

According to Kylee Baumle, "As an adult, summer generations of monarchs will live anywhere from two to six weeks, if they live out their natural life and manage to avoid predators."[3] Only two to six weeks is a short life! Almost instantly after birth, these black-veined beauties prepare to give birth to the next generation. Can you imagine that the job of these short-lived generations is simply to lay the foundation for the next generation? Then it happens. Standing upon the foundation of what has gone before, the fourth generation is birthed, ready to take flight. This generation, the final generation of the summer, is called the Methuselah Generation. Like Methuselah from the Bible, this generation is known for exceptionally long life.[4]

There are other unique aspects about this migrating generation. They are slightly bigger and stronger. This enables them to make their long migratory flight. The monarch's migration is truly extraordinary: "A butterfly born in Canada or the U.S. begins an epic journey of up to 2,800 miles

---

3   Baumle, *The Monarch*, 28.
4   Methuselah, who lived 969 years, is mentioned twice in biblical genealogies and in Genesis 5:21–27. The generations before him did not live that long; the generations after him did not live that long.

south to a place they've never been before."[5] What courage! They do not logically know where they are going. And yet they set out on a magnificent pilgrimage.

What influences the migrating generation to begin their long trek across the country? There are both internal and external influences that signal the Divine time to embark on this impressive journey. Internally, while being formed within the chrysalis, the Methuselah monarch is created with a lower level of hormones that stimulate its reproductive behavior. This alone extends the butterfly's life. They do not mate until they reach their destination in Mexico.

Another external trigger is the monarch butterfly's cold-bloodedness and the effect of the outside temperature: "When the angle of the sun reaches 57° off the horizon, the monarch knows that migration is to commence. Simultaneously, the days are also gradually becoming shorter ... this variant is important. Consecutive days of the same short length will not trigger migration; ever-shortening day length seems to be the most important determining factor for migration to begin."[6]

What strength of heart and stamina it takes for the little monarch to fly such a long distance! Of course, there are way stations for rest along the way. Kylee Baumle, in her book that I cite throughout, provides fantastic instruction on how to create a safe, sacred space for the migrating monarchs.[7]

On their flight toward new beginnings, butterflies often join together. These groups of monarchs frequently feed along the way. It is so surprising to me that the migratory butterflies arrive in Mexico weighing more than when they left![8] If the weather turns cold or rainy, the migration is paused until the sun shines and warms their black veins so that they may continue flight. As I pray with this image of the feasting butterfly gaining great endurance, strength, and stamina for the transfiguring journey and resting in the cool temperatures in northern Mexico, my mind turns to the soul-feast nourishing the potential within, provided to us in and through training in spiritual direction.

The premise of this book is that, like the caterpillar, the church and its leaders are in the process of metamorphosis. God's bounty nourishes our interior life. The old passes away so that the new beauty of divine creation

---

5   Baumle, *The Monarch*, 35.
6   Baumle, *The Monarch*, 37.
7   Baumle, *The Monarch*, "Creating a Monarch Way Station," 105ff.
8   Baumle, *The Monarch*, 38.

may be birthed. Like the caterpillar, we too have a hunger deep within that urges us into the mystery of transfiguration. Yet, the wonder crosses my heart: What causes us to pause on The Way? Even though the transfiguring process of spiritual formation happens individually and within each generation, are there historical eras that lay a foundation for just the right moment for God's spiritual awakening?

Like the migrating monarch, the fullness of the beauty of the church is built upon generations that have gone before us. This is exemplified as we celebrate and hold the wisdom of teachers of years gone by. However, unlike the butterfly, we also can place many stipulations and resistances on this transfiguring process. Questions arise: Do congregations or leaders ever hark back to days gone by, longing for comfort of the known and familiar ways of faith? Does fear ever rise up, casting a shadow on ethical behaviors striving to maintain control over a process beyond human grasp? Are we ever afraid of the unknown? Could competing voices within the church give rise to confusion? Are there outcries from the tradition of church naming that the metamorphosis of transfiguring community is more than we ever bargained for?

As we look at church history, each time the generation for awakening stirs the waters of tradition, God urges openness within humanity toward God's newest possibility of living the Third Way of the resurrected Jesus. Through the art of spiritual direction in its many forms—individual, group, and corporate influence—is it possible that we, the church and its leaders, like a chrysalis, may become transparent enough for all to see God's Divine beauty?

Internal yearnings cause us to plumb the depths of Scripture, weave the cultural context through God's heart, and feel driven to articulate new ways of being church together. Are we brave enough to explore them? Could some outside triggers for church—a pandemic, sexual abuse scandals, systemic racism, slippery slopes of ethical decline, rigidity of extreme right or left political and theological positions, and waning participation—signal our internal searching for the Divine? How does your heart burn with desire to notice God's power and presence even more profoundly, personally, and corporately through the shifting tides of culture?

Just as the butterfly pauses on the migration toward new possibility born from their stay in the cool climate of Mexico, so you are invited to pause. The first Spiritual Direction Readiness Assessment and Congregational Examen provides an opportunity to chew upon, digest, and consider how God is present within life. In this historical era of spiritual awakening, the tools of spiritual training and spiritual direction may in fact be one avenue to accompany us along the descending formational way toward greater Christlikeness.

The Beauty of Becoming: Spiritual Formation

As much as we may like our position in life, the truth is we have not yet arrived. We live, like the life cycle of the emerging butterfly, a life of process. We are constantly being shaped by events, experiences, images, desires, and cultural norms. World events such as pandemics, wars, financial crises, social injustices of racism, prejudice, terrorism, poverty, and displacement of individuals weigh heavily on us. The tides of mass media influence our awareness. We are formed by influences from within and beyond ourselves. It is into this environment that we are gifted with the process of becoming even more of our authentic beauty. This is the *Imago Dei*, the image of God imprinted within us at our physical birth.

It is not a question of *if* we are formed, but rather *what* influences shape our individual lives and the communal life of a congregation. A question akin to this one is *how* are we being influenced by God? Robert Mulholland Jr. wrote in his book *Shaped by the Word*,

> Human life is, by its very nature, spiritual formation. The question is not *whether* to undertake spiritual formation. The question is *what kind* of spiritual formation are we already engaged in? Are we being increasingly conformed to the brokenness and disintegration of the world, or are we being increasingly conformed to the wholeness and integration of the image of Christ?[9]

"When the final molt begins, . . . They will hang limp and twisted in spiral. Soon the caterpillar will begin contracting; just behind the head, the skin will split open to reveal the emerald green chrysalis. Contractions continue, with the old skin proceeding to be split and shoved up, accordion style, towards the top."

Baumle, *The Monarch*, 24–25.

---

9   Robert Mulholland Jr. 2002. *Shaped by the Word*. Nashville, TN: Upper Room Publishers. Page 26.

As Christians we consent to this God-shaping energy. It is God's presence that actively creates and transforms thoughts, attitudes, and actions for loving self, others, and God. Mulholland's definition of Christian spiritual formation is "the process of being more nearly conformed to the image of Christ for the sake of others."[10] This process is not something that happens overnight. It is a lifelong shaping toward Christlikeness. Incrementally, we become living witnesses of God's power and presence in the world. Much like the metamorphosis of the caterpillar, God's formation of new life shines forth through humanity.

Spiritual direction assists seekers' descent on the formational spiral with the ebb and flow of energy and God-presence going back and forth between seeker and God. A hand-drawn tornado depicts the descending way toward God's heart. With each descending cycle, we are wooed toward union with Divine Love. As we live this formational spiral, we are invited to consent to God as the greatest influence upon our collective and individual minds and hearts. It is our consent that opens the way for becoming more Christlike.

Under the Umbrella

Spiritual formation is like a large umbrella overarching private and corporate ministries. Ministries of worship, prayer, small groups, acts of mercy, justice (within and beyond the congregation), and hospitality all have the potential for spiritual formation. The foundation of spiritual formation for ministry enfolds every aspect of both private and corporate ministry. Also under the umbrella of spiritual formation are the soul-care ministries of pastoral care, spiritual direction, spiritual friendship, and mentoring. To envision how these ministries are interconnected, please see figure 1. The foundational tools of spiritual direction training potentially undergird all aspects of congregational ministry under the umbrella of spiritual formation. This is the foundation of all private and corporate ministries. These ministries range from administration, evangelism, hospitality, education, preaching, and soul-care roles and functions within the church.

---

10 Mulholland, *Shaped by the Word*, 25.

Figure 1. The Umbrella of Spiritual Formation

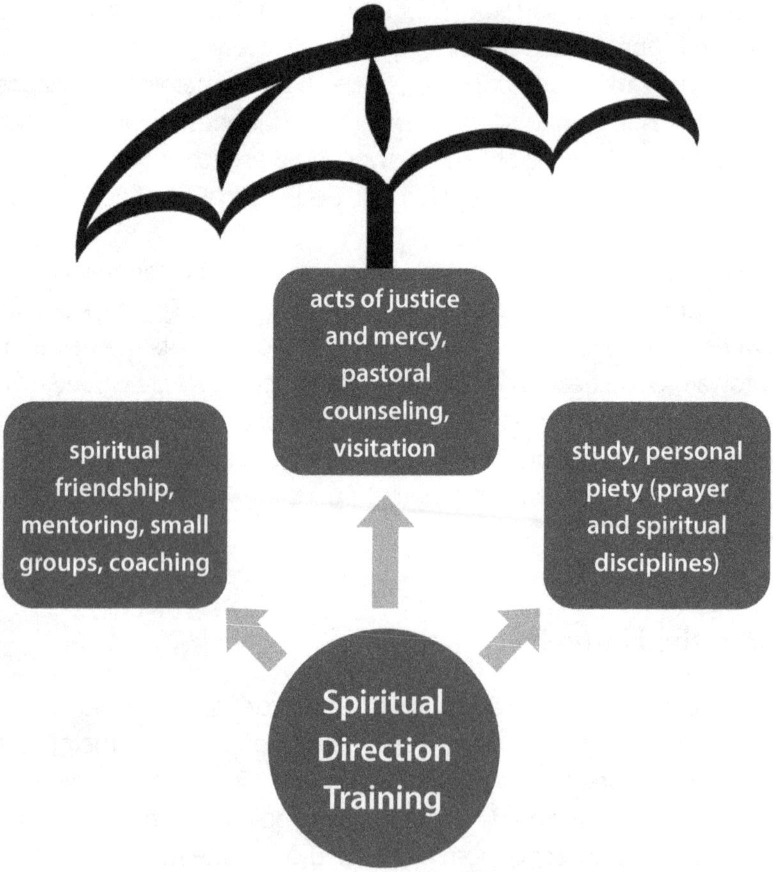

Since the focus of this book is how spiritual direction and its training tools ignite the metamorphic process of transfiguration within and through the church, I will turn to the basic dynamics of spiritual direction with the use of three-way listening.

Three-Way Listening

Three-way listening, a technique used in spiritual direction, is when two or more persons listen to each other and to God. This is a listening triangle of love among listener, speaker, and God, as depicted in figure 2.

Three-way listening occurs when all three—God, directee, and spiritual director—listen to one another. The director listens to the other individual and to God. The directee, the one sharing his or her story and seeking deep-ened awareness of God, is listening to the director and to God. God is lis-tening and whispering to both director and directee. The one sharing the story may find it harder to listen to God while speaking. The director is the intentional God-listener.

Theological and biblical understanding for three-way listening is the foundation of the ministry of Christian spiritual direction. God is a com-municating God. God yearns to speak, listen, and, by the power of God's Word, create new life. Speaking is such a powerful mode of presence for God that the world itself, according to Genesis, was spoken into being.[11] God did not stop communicating with this one sole expression of the Word as we read in Genesis 1. The Gospel of John also tells us that it was God's Word that became incarnate in human life. That life was Jesus. To become incarnate is the expression of God's Word living or indwelling human life (John 1:1–3a, 14a).

Figure 2. Three-Way Listening

God

Spiritual Direction

Directee or Speaker   Spiritual Director/Listener

---

11 "In the beginning when God created the heavens and the earth, the earth was a formless void and darkness covered the face of the deep, while a wind from God swept over the face of the waters. Then God said, . . ." (Gen 1:1–3 NRSV).

This communicating God, who creates by speaking and who became human in Jesus, provides one more mode of communicating God's Word to God's people. After the death and resurrection of Jesus, the resurrected Jesus came and stood among them (John 20). It was there in the upper room with the doors locked that the Third Way of communicating with God's people began. On the breath of life, the Word of God resounds through the Holy Spirit to each individual and to all generations.

This three-way expression of God's Word speaking is known theologically as the Trinity. It is here in the fullness of the Trinity that three-way listening is born. God's Word continually whispers, sometimes shouts, to God's creation. God yearns to influence and guide, encourage, and form our lives. This *is* the process of Christian spiritual formation that Robert Mulholland Jr. articulated. This is an inward transforming power of God's creative Word that transfigures the heart into a more Christlike nature. This process of metamorphosis is the desired hope of a spiritually formed life and community.

"Once the cremaster is firmly embedded, writhing and twisting continues until the old skin falls off and the chrysalis hangs only by the cremaster. In the next couple of hours, the new chrysalis will shrink a bit and take on the traditional shape and will begin to harden."

Baumle, *The Monarch*, 25–26.

Like the caterpillar hidden within the chrysalis, the energy, presence, and power of God's Word deeply forms human life from the inside of our being to our outside actions. This is not a once-in-a-lifetime event. Through attentive prayer, holy listening, and openness within the human heart, God's Word continues to form us into God's new creation throughout our lifetime.

Those open to this life-shaping presence and energy of God are transfigured into even more of God's Christlikeness. Like the metamorphosis of the caterpillar turning into the butterfly, the old is gone and a new way of life is birthed. However, sadly, this process of God's action within human life is often met with resistance, fear, rejection, and apathy. (Resistances to the spiritually formed life will be discussed in section 3.) Openness to God is prayer.

Spiritual Direction as Prayer

St. Augustine states, "At its deepest level, prayer has to do with the longing to be in union with God, to live in the reality of God."[12] Prayer is like breathing. Through prayer we take in the life-creating breath of God and expel all that keeps us from God. Prayer means being filled with the presence of the resurrected Jesus in mystical union with God. "We are meant to pray. . . . I can hold my breath only for so long before I must take another breath."[13] Prayer is our response and God's initiative to the deep hunger within. Spiritual direction raises our conscious awareness of this symbiotic communion.

As God prays within us through three-way listening, God becomes the true spiritual director. The director simply becomes the transparent vessel for focusing on God's Word and prayer during the conversation. It is not the spiritual director's job to influence theological perspective, set the directee straight, give advice, or fix the tenderhearted client. At its best, spiritual direction is prayer. Spiritual direction as lived prayer is not only a mode of conversation, an art that enlarges articulation of God and the prayer-heart of the directee, but it is a safe, sacred space to experience God's presence. It is the holy ground of prayer lived in community.

Spiritual direction "is most interested in what happens when a person consciously puts himself [or herself] into the presence of God."[14] Historically, this has been one-on-one conversations. However, small groups may incorporate spiritual direction, as can the corporate arenas of church. (These will be discussed in section 5.) Whether individually, within groups, or corporately, spiritual direction is a mode of listening that has distinctive characteristics for opening new contemplative ways of experiencing God, self, and the other.

It is essential to hold lightly and with high regard the one coming for spiritual direction. The spiritual director is literally called to see Christ in the other by honoring him, her, or them with clear boundaries and strong ethical integrity: "When both director and directee are mutually obedient and engaged in holy listening, the story gets told."[15]

---

12 Jim Forest. 2006. *Praying with Icons*. New York: Orbis Books. Page 31.
13 Forest, *Praying with Icons*, 30.
14 William A. Barry and William J. Connolly. 2009. *The Practice of Spiritual Direction*. Revised and updated edition. San Francisco: HarperCollins Publishers. Page 8.
15 Margaret Guenther. 1992. *Holy Listening: The Art of Spiritual Direction*. Boston: Cowley Publications. Pages 88, 91, 144.

> "When [the monarchs] take flight in the fall, do they know
> how very far their journey will eventually take them? Or are
> they simply answering a call within themselves . . . ?"
>
> Baumle, *The Monarch*, 36.

Wonders rise within my spirit. Has our rushed pace caused us to lose the passion for slowly traversing the formational spiral toward union with God? What if we, the church and its leaders, have become stuck in habitual ways of praying? If so, does this limit our anticipation of God's possibility for vibrant life? Could the process of metamorphosis—that is, becoming transfigured into greater Christlikeness—become stymied? Like the monarch butterfly awaiting the fourth generation to traverse new ground, does the church ever build upon, shatter, or reshape what has come before it? Our continued discovery of this transfiguring metamorphosis in the contemplative tradition turns toward historic leaders and the wild wilderness of culture in section 2 as we discern wisdom for response to these questions. First, we pause for inward assessment and examen.

Spiritual Direction Readiness Assessment and Congregational Examen

At the end of each section of this book is a Spiritual Direction Readiness Assessment and Congregational Examen. Consider creating a portfolio, either on the computer or with pencil and paper. Within this portfolio, record your responses to the assessment and examen. At the end of this book, review your portfolio of responses. Ponder how God is inviting you further into the metamorphosis process personally and within the church.

WORKSHEET OF ASSESSMENT AND EXAMEN

Personal Leadership Assessment

A. Describe your inward hunger.

B. What is your heart's deepest longing?

C. With whom do you speak of your internal yearnings and faith?

D. When have you experienced three-way listening with God and another? What is that like for you?

E. What is it like for you to take intentional pause from daily busyness?

F. As you ponder the metamorphosis process of the caterpillar, consider how this relates to your experience. Review the stages of the caterpillar's metamorphosis. In what stage do you find yourself living at this moment?

    a. *The egg stage of spiritual life.* How have or are you experiencing new beginning in the spiritual life?

    b. *Larva or caterpillar stage of spiritual life.* There is a deep hunger within. Are you wandering across the same terrain of faith looking to be nourished in the same ways? How do you pause to be solely nourished by God's bounty?

    c. *Pupa or chrysalis stage I of spiritual life.* Consider times you have hunkered down in place and waited. Perhaps you have experienced stay-at-home orders through a pandemic. How did you live the issues of these orders as an invitation from God? What is it like for you in the stillness of God's transforming womb? How do you wait? What do you notice?

    d. *Chrysalis stage II: The mysterious and hidden inward yearning and formation in the spiritual life.* What is it like for you to wait in stillness and silence? How are you noticing God's energy, presence, and powerful Spirit at work within you, even though everything on the outside may appear exactly as it was before? How is God preparing you for new life? What is this inward process of transformation like for you?

e. *Butterfly stage I: Transfiguration, becoming the beautiful new life of God, yet still constrained.* The monarch's chrysalis now is transparent, so all on the outside can view the beautiful new life hanging upside down. The butterfly is not yet set free for flight. Ponder hesitancies of the heart you may experience as you imagine your new life. When have you felt constrained, not able to truly be the fullness of who God created you to be?

f. *Butterfly stage II: Emergence of new life ready for new spiritual flight.* When and how have you experienced new birthing of God? What is it like for you to be set free from constraints and live as Jesus' loves? Imagine being totally unrestrained to love. What does it feel like to live such unrestrained freedom of God's love? How do others around you react when you test your spiritual wings to take flight in living deeply from God's *Imago Dei* from within?

Please close your time of prayer with this or one of your own prayers.

Holy God, One in Three and Three in One, I love you. You know the struggles of my heart as I yearn for expanded awareness of you. I didn't even know that I was yearning so deeply. Accept my yearnings and open my heart so that I may live as you love among your people. Grant me freedom to release what holds me captive and move into your greatest desires. May I become new, as I live, love, and dance with the fullness of your spirit in relationship with our neighbors. Amen.

Congregational Examen

A. Describe the congregational heart yearning.
B. What is the congregation's deepest collective soul-desire?
C. Who are the sacred persons creating safe space of listening for the congregation?
D. How many people participate in three-way listening conversations?
E. What is it like for the congregation to take intentional pauses from the busyness of church life?

F. As you ponder the metamorphosis process of the caterpillar, consider how this relates to the church. Has the church become new after reopening from shutdowns related to the pandemic? What influence has civil protest had upon the church? Review the stages of the caterpillar's metamorphosis. What stage do you find the congregation living at this moment?

    a. *The egg stage of spiritual life.* How has the congregation been experiencing new beginning in the spiritual life?

    b. *Larva or caterpillar stage of spiritual life.* There is a deep hunger within. Is the congregation wandering across the same terrain of faith looking to be nourished in the same ways? How does the congregation pause to be solely nourished by God's bounty?

    c. *Pupa or chrysalis stage I of spiritual life.* Consider times the congregation has hunkered down in place and waited. How did the congregation live the issues of pandemic-related stay-at-home orders as an invitation from God? What is it like for the congregation to wait in the stillness of God's transforming womb? How does the congregation wait?

    d. *Chrysalis stage II: The mysterious and hidden inward yearning and formation in the spiritual life.* As the congregation waits in stillness and silence, how do parishioners notice God's energy, presence, and powerful Spirit at work, even though everything on the outside may appear exactly as it was before? How is God preparing the congregation for new life?

    e. *Butterfly stage I: Transfiguration, becoming the beautiful new life of God, yet still constrained.* The monarch's chrysalis now is transparent, so all on the outside can view the beautiful new life hanging upside down. The butterfly is not yet set free for flight. Ponder hesitancies of the congregation for new life. When has the congregation felt constrained, not able to truly be the fullness of who God created it to be?

    f. *Butterfly stage II: Emergence of new life ready for new spiritual flight.* When and how has the congregation experienced new birthing of God? What is it like to be set free from constraints and live as Jesus' loves? Imagine being totally unrestrained to love. How do others around the congregation react when parishioners test new spiritual wings to take flight in living deeply as *Imago Dei?*

Interface of Personal and Congregational Responses

A. Are the leader and congregation in the same position of transfiguring metamorphosis?
B. What is similar between the leader and congregation?
C. What is different between the leader and congregation?
D. How is the heart hungering together as leader and congregation for more than is currently experienced?

Please close your time of prayer with this or one of your own prayers.

> Holy God, One in Three and Three in One, we love you. You know the struggles of our heart as we yearn for expanded awareness of you traversing the spiral of formation toward union with your heart. We didn't even know that we were yearning so deeply within. Accept our intent and desire to open our heart so that we may live as you love in community and among your people. Grant our congregation freedom to release what holds it captive and move into your greatest desires. Together may we become new as we live, love, and dance with the fullness of your spirit in relationship with our neighbors. Amen.

Two

THE WILD WILDERNESS

The Caterpillar Stage of Spiritual Life

Kylee Baumle notes, "Being invertebrates, monarch caterpillars have an exo-skeleton that doesn't stretch or grow much, so they must shed it periodically as they outgrow it. This is called molting."[1] I am amazed that the caterpillar literally walks out of its skin. The caterpillar is not passive during the molting. It must be intentional to move. The caterpillar's job is to eat, grow, and prepare for new birth.

It is the job of every leader to feast upon God's soul-nourishing presence. The focus of this section is on the leader. I wonder if in the process of becoming more Christlike we have molting growth like the caterpillar. How does our faith experience and understanding of God stretch to new capacity? We are invited to walk out of the old and into the new.

The caterpillar stage of the spiritual life highlights hunger and the invitation to molt. You, the leader, may not even know you are hungering for God, but restlessness burns within your heart. You may find yourself wandering into places and spaces of faith that you never anticipated going. You may feel driven by an interior love to keep spiraling toward the Trinity of God's heart. The leader in pursuit of lifelong metamorphosis finds his or her

---

1   Kylee Baumle. 2017. *The Monarch: Saving Our Most-Loved Butterfly.* Pittsburgh, PA: St. Lynn's Press. Page 21.

journey is not just for the leader alone. Many times, like the four spiritual giants discussed in this section, a deep hunger rises within, which compels the leader to share the tools of spiritual direction training with others. Are you willing to step out of the old and into the new?

The Wild Wilderness of Culture

Section 2 takes us into the wild wilderness of culture. From disorientation, chaos, and confusion to unleashed, illuminating God-possibility, we get a glimpse of historical discovery. History shows faith-wisdom giants who, like the caterpillar, shed the old and grew into new wineskins (Mark 2:21–22). Harking back to intentionally Spirit-formed and Spirit-led leaders from the margins, we discover those who inspired others toward the edge of God's new era of faith formation.

The four faith giants highlighted provide foundational examples of tools from spiritual direction training that open the way for spiritual metamorphosis within personal, then subsequently communal, life. This created spiritual awakenings within each historical period. History bears witness that spiritual direction training has structure and form for deepening and expanding awareness of God amid chaos. With the *ammas* and *abbas* (the desert spiritual mothers and fathers)—St. Benedict, St. Ignatius, and Rev. John Wesley—we wonder if we too could open the way for the metamorphosis of church with spiritual awakening.

Why did these faith-wisdom leaders seek new faith practices and deepened ways to share God's presence? Much like the maturing caterpillar, they were personally compelled from the mysterious power within. The result? They passionately sought spiritual discovery as they grew in wisdom of God. When leaders' hunger for God was met through deepened search for God, they too, like the caterpillar, outgrew old ways of prayer and walked into the spiral descent of God's formation.

As their spiritual awareness, experience, and understanding of God amid humanity's disorientation stretched beyond its former thinking and doing, their personal wineskins of faith were stretched. This continually expanded their spiritual conversation and prayer. Humbled by God's amazing power and presence, they felt compelled to share ever-deepening spiritual practices with others.

As the leaders' spirit was ignited by the passionate love of God through God's spiritual guidance, their brilliance of faith could not be contained. Akin to the caterpillar's molting, the culture of their time and place became restrictive, limiting movement on the formational spiral toward the heart of God.

The desert *abbas* and *ammas* tried to escape the disorientation of culture by going into the desert for solitude. The rugged, arid terrain taught them great reliance on God. They learned to hear beyond presentation of wind and dust to God's whispering heart. However, they were often not alone in the desert. Seekers came out to converse with them in search of God-wisdom and guidance. None of them acted solely for their own formation.

St. Benedict was one of those early *abbas*. Those who sought him often stayed in community with him. Because Benedict experienced firsthand the struggles with cultural disorientation and temptations, he knew from the inside of his being to his outside actions how intentional one must be in seeking ever-deepening relationship with God. He wrote *The Rule of Life* for those living in community with him at the monastery.[2]

St. Ignatius gives us a historic glimpse of the culture and discontented chaos of the Middle Ages. Even though he began his own private faith exploration through a convalescent period after a military injury, he too was compelled to write. The *Spiritual Exercises* deepen God-listening skills while they examine daily life.[3] This is a gift for those seeking a structured exploration of God through spiritual direction.

Rev. John Wesley never had any intention of starting a new faith movement. Following in his father's footsteps and learning on the knee of his mother, the gospel message seeped deeply into his heart. After crossing the ocean with a group of Moravians and marveling at the stability of their faith amid a raging storm, John claimed his yearning within. Once his heart was "strangely warmed" after an intimate experience of God's nearness and power, he felt the desire to write, preach, and share his methodical passion for spiritually forming prayer, worship, and justice.

Why highlight these giants of faith? The soul of the churches affected by these leaders was phenomenal. These historic leaders provide a guide for us as we seek to implement spiritual direction training as a pathway for

2   *St. Benedict's Rule for Monasteries.* Translated from the Latin by Leonard J. Doyle. Collegeville, MN: Liturgical Press. Available online at http://www.gutenberg.org/files/50040/50040-h/50040-h.html.

3   Barbara Bedolla and Domini Totro, SJ. 1990. "Ignatian Spirituality." In *Spiritual Traditions for the Contemporary Church*, edited by R. Maas and G. O'Donnell, OP. Nashville, TN: Abingdon Press. Pages 172–73.

the metamorphosis in the church. The urgency of this need resounds as people rebuild lives after the first wave of the COVID-19 pandemic and as people protest systemic racism and injustice. In our brief overview of these historic leaders, we will experience foundational tools of spiritual direction training. As you read their stories, consider what themes, practices, passions, disciplines, and God-energy they exemplify to which your spirit is drawn. You and I have the potential, by God's grace, to share faith-wisdom like these saints who have gone before us. But before we move to the first historical figures from the desert, together we pause to learn the three molting movements of a spiritual awakening.

Spiritual Awakening

What is a spiritual awakening, and how does it come about? Glenn Hinson suggests there are three phases that categorize spiritual awakenings: disorientation, heightened religious search, and change of consciousness.[4] There is not a smooth, one-time transition between these phases of awakening. As individuals and communities go through the painful time of disorientation, they move back and forth through these periods. It is when many people are living into new ways of thinking, embodying faith, and prayer that the awakened state is realized.

For both personal and communal awakening, there is energetic spiraling toward the heart of God with these three distinct movements. Disorientation and chaos occur when old wineskins have grown too tight. Personally, individuals feel very restricted and overwhelmed. When these overwhelmed persons gather in community, congregational chaos may ensue.

This congregational chaos is also perceived in the community at large beyond the church in a period of disorientation. Pandemics, wars, or oppressive regimes might be prominent. Fear becomes a dominant force in making choices or justifying persecution and prejudgments of others. People become restlessness as they live through injustice in social systems while financial indexes fluctuate frequently. Cultural values, belief systems, theological positioning, and politics often seem at odds with one another. Many voices might be vying for attention during a chaotic time. Each voice claims to have the "correct" solution to the chaos that seeks to reign supremely.

---

4   Buckwell, *Rediscovering*, 2007.

James Melvin Washington describes contemporary culture as such: "We have become the servants of an instant gratification that is devoid of both thought and purpose. We are hurriers with narcissistic agendas who refuse to look for [God] in the groans, joys, and plight of the poor."[5] Washington goes on to name the spiritual malaise that results from such a harried time: "One reality is that far too many of us do miss [God]. We yearn to feel [God's] presence. But we do not comprehend the nature of this absence which we often call 'emptiness.' We have been absent from [God] for so long that we either never knew, or have forgotten, that the soul must be nurtured and nourished. Spiritual malnutrition besets us."[6] How often we search the refrigerator when we feel the need for something, even if we are not hungry. Or we may reach for a mind- and emotion-altering alcoholic drink or drugs. Have we become so accustomed to the emptiness within that we would do almost anything to cover it up? It is into disoriented culture that the urgency for spiritual direction training is heightened. The heart-clarifying conversation with three-way listening opens the way for God's new possibility.

Deep within the caterpillar an innate force pulls it toward transfiguring silence. In the depth of God's womb, the creative Word of God forms a marvelous new life.

Contemplative listening through spiritual direction could transform the landscape of the church. The question becomes, Are we willing to move from our old ways of doing and walk into God's new way of being? This opens the way for the second molting of our wineskins in the process of spiritual awakening. We move into a time of deepened religious search as our broken heart compels us to look beyond what is currently being experienced.

A Heart Broken Open to Unleash New Possibility

The caterpillar wasn't birthed to stay on the ground. It was meant for flight. The monarch caterpillar sheds its skin four times during its life. With each new skin its potential for flight incrementally is unleashed beyond imagined

---

5   James Melvin Washington. 1994. *Conversations with God: Two Centuries of Prayers by African Americans*. New York: HarperPerennial. Pages 283–84.

6   Washington, *Conversations with God*, 283.

possibility. The process of metamorphosis begins with the willingness to be open to change and formation.

Change itself may be disorienting. Through times of disorientation, the heart can break. Sometimes when the heart breaks it splinters into shards of pointed anger, violence, and vengeances. These sharp points of pain and brokenness threaten to harm all who are in its way. Others enter the pain and woundedness of heartbreak and disorientation in a way that allows the pain to become our greatest teacher.

The broken heart that does not run from the pain but seeks it to become our teacher learns to embrace the wisdom of suffering. This heart finds itself broken all the way open. This broken-all-the-way-open heart enters the second phase of spiritual awakening: heightened religious search. The heart becomes a place of fertile ground for new birthing. The open heart, now pierced with possibility, experiences contemplative seeing beyond the surface presentation of disarray. Tentatively at first, and then more assuredly, the seeker steps deeper into new possibility. This step into heightened religious search may or may not be within organized religion. In fact, often the institutional church is the last to know that an awakening is underway.

The third phase of awakening is the change of consciousness. It is the result of the final molting of old wineskins. Through many spiritual direction conversations with attention to regular rhythms of spiritual disciplines, the old ways of thinking, feeling, and destressing are transformed into new possibility. The new transformed possibility is much more than revival or renewal. This transfiguration of people from chaos to the new opens the way to live God's luminous love collectively shining forth from the awakened soul of the congregation.

"When the caterpillar molts, it will stop feeding, and will remain still for many hours before beginning the process. The outer skin separates from the inner, with the aid of an enzyme that starts to dissolve the outer skin. The caterpillar . . . literally walk[s] out of its old skin, and most times will eat it, thus taking advantage of the nutrients it still contains."

Baumle, *The Monarch*, 22.

The wonder returns about our contemporary culture. Are we in the midst of a spiritual awakening? Assessment of our current time shows many who are overwhelmed, grieving, struggling with divisions among God's people, experiencing immigration oppression, and paralyzed with fear. From the 9/11 terror attacks, to ever-increasing random acts of violence at school, shopping centers, places of worship, and sporting events, to pandemics and protests, people are experiencing disorientation. Chaos is escalated by the ever-present daily stressors of overextended and exhausted workers, parents, preachers, teachers, and schoolchildren. Now is the time to learn from the wise elders of our spiritual past.

Through the historic lens of ancient prayer practices from the early *ammas* and *abbas* of the desert, St. Benedict, St. Ignatius, and Rev. John Wesley, we experience the foundation of spiritual direction. Historically, intentional heightened search for God spawns spiritual awakenings. Could these foundational spiritual direction training tools gift us with a transfiguring metamorphosis in the church also? I trust so.

Wisdom from the Past

The Desert Ammas *and* Abbas

Why would anyone leave the comfort of home and family to live a life of struggle and food insecurity? Early spiritual fathers and mothers of Christianity did just that. The *abbas* and *ammas* intentionally made themselves vulnerable to the elements of weather, isolation, and desert creatures. The reality of God's provisions under harsh conditions spurred them toward an ever-deepened experience of God. Their intentionality caused them to become known as wisdom persons of faith.

Pilgrims from the cities sought out the *ammas* and *abbas*. These early spiritual directors gently shepherded people into new awareness of God's guidance and God's active and loving presence in their lives. Two of the foundational tools for spiritual direction training used by the *ammas* and *abbas* were silence and solitude. Two spiritual disciplines that deepened silence and solitude were "the cell" and "give me a word."

A famous wisdom saying from the desert says, "Go and sit in your cell. It will teach you all you need to know." Not only did the cell reference going to a quiet place, but most important, the cell referred to the interior sacred space within the human heart. When a pilgrim was told to return to his or her cell, it was an invitation to look deeply within one's self and seek the authentic self's truest image of Christ.[7] This takes courage and intentionality, and is often aided by companions gifted with the skill of three-way listening.

When pilgrims came to the desert elder seeking God's presence and guidance, they would often ask for a word. This became the spiritual discipline of "give me a word." "The word was often a short phrase to nourish and challenge the receiver. The word was meant to be wrestled with and slowly grown into."[8] As the seeker sought to understand, internalize, and live from this word, God's presence shaped interior character, attitudes, and mannerisms into greater Christlikeness.

Assumptions of prayerfulness and God's formative presence were never an option. We too must become intentional in our seeking like the disciples who sought wisdom in the desert. It takes intention to show up, especially coming from a contemporary posture of individualized faith. With the intention of spiritual direction, the leader moves through disorientation, doubts, fears, and hopes to discover greater illumination of God's presence. Even during the best-of-faith times, there is more to be experienced and known of God, which can be discovered with intentional spiritual direction.

Monthly spiritual direction conversations provide a sacred, safe space similar to the cell. Taking the intentional hour away from the harried pace of life opens one to greater awareness of God. Regularly coming to a spirit-filled space brings peace to the weary soul. In the cell, that sacred space for spiritual direction, the leader can be attentive to the present moment and breathe God. Upon leaving that space, the leader carries with him or her the interior stillness of God into his or her everyday life and leadership.

The wonder of how silence and solitude could affect people today in the hectic pace of life is vital to ponder. Often, we are afraid of too much silence because we do not like the thoughts, feelings, and emotional memories that drift through our minds. The discipline of "give me a word" from desert wisdom provides focus and opens space within the brain for God's formative shaping. "Give me a word" has morphed over the years into such prayer practices as centering prayer, mantras, and breath prayer.[9]

---

7   Brenda Buckwell. 2019. "Your Lenten Discovery Toward Resurrection: The Resounding Word." Unpublished manuscript.

8   Christine Valters Paintner. 2012. *Desert Fathers and Mothers: Early Christian Wisdom Sayings*. Woodstock, VT: Skylight Paths Publishing. Page 2.

9   Mantras and centering prayers both utilize a single-word focus in prayer. The intention of how the word is used differs between these two prayer techniques. Mantras focus the prayer on repetition of the prayer word, which draws the pray-er into deeper union with God. In centering prayer, the prayer word is used to refocus

Pause and Ponder

We conclude this section on influences of the desert elders with a wisdom saying from Abba Joseph. Abba Joseph gifts us with an image of transfiguration as he encourages love of Christ within and through the leader.

> Abba Lot went to see Abba Joseph and he said to him, "Abba, as far as I can, I say my little office, I fast a little, I pray and meditate, I live in peace and as far as I can I purify my thoughts. What else can I do?" Then the old man stood up and stretched his hands toward heaven; his fingers became like ten lamps of fire and he said to him, "If you will, you can become all flame." God, the Divine energy, is Love. Meditation will lead us to experience this love deeply within our own being and we too will be transformed by it.[10]

Pause now and ponder desert wisdom foundational to spiritual direction.

Still your mind and heart this day. Take a few deep breaths; inhale the power and presence of God, and exhale all that is resistant and overextended within you. Once you have calmed your interior heart, ponder these questions:

- What is your experience of silence?
- Imagine in your mind's eye that you are sitting with an *amma* or *abba*. When you ask him or her for a word, what response do you hear?

---

the mind and heart when distraction intrudes silence. The centering word pushes the other thoughts out of mind. Thomas Keating has written widely on centering prayer. A resource book is: Keating. 2006. *Open Mind, Open Heart*. 20th anniversary edition. New York: Continuum.

Breath prayer is a six- to eight-syllable phrase that focuses mind and heart's attention on God. The pray-er breathes in and mentally thinks the prayer phrase. On the exhale, the pray-er releases all that keeps the pray-er from entering more fully into God's presence. Ron DelBene, an Episcopal priest, first introduced me to breath prayer. A resource book is: Ron DelBene, with Mary and Herb Montgomery. 1995. *The Hunger of the Heart*. Nashville, TN: Upper Room Books.

10 Brenda Buckwell. 2016. *The Advent of God's Word: Listening for the Power of the Divine Whisper*. Woodstock, VT: Skylight Paths Publishing. Page 146.

- As you sit with the desert elder, slowly contemplate the word that comes to you. You may choose to journal that word over and over across the page, allowing it to soak deep within your heart.
- What is it like for you to sit silently before God with your word?
- Once you have had as much time as you desire with your word, reread Abba Joseph's words.
- How do you feel about becoming all fire?

May the Pentecostal passion of Jesus' transfiguring Spirit anoint your life this day.

Why not become all fire with the passion of God? Does the caterpillar ever desire to turn back? Does the caterpillar ever profess it has had enough change and doesn't move forward in the process of molting? I wonder how the caterpillar leads us too in wisdom for new awakening. "When the caterpillar molts, something must secure the old skin, allowing the monarch to walk out of it. Prior to molting the caterpillar uses its spinneret located just below its mouth to lay down a light layer of silk strands. . . . This holds the old skin in place as the caterpillar walks out of it."

Baumle, *The Monarch*, 22.

In the wild wilderness of the desert and arid spaces of cultural chaos, the process of metamorphosis begins. It was not the resuscitation of the church that the *ammas* and *abbas* sought, but the total inward transfiguring gift of the Holy Spirit. The art of spiritual direction burst forth into passionate flame, illuminating our unique place within the world.

St. Benedict, Abba from the Desert

St. Benedict gifts us with the foundational wisdom for spiritual direction through regular and rhythmic practice of the spiritual disciplines. He required each of the monks within his community to meet regularly for spiritual direction. Between sessions the monks were to attend to their own practices of prayer. Prayer was to be a way of life. Whether the monks were eating, working, reading, studying, or conversing with others, all these actions were to become prayer. This single-minded focus is challenging to our contemporary dualistic mindset.

Single-minded focus. That is almost a foreign concept to the multitasking, hyper-speed, instantaneous technological culture of our day. Often a nod is given to God with opening invocations and closing prayers at events and business meetings in both secular and sacred settings. The sacred portion of life is frequently delegated to worship gatherings, time in nature, and morning and evening devotions. These are fantastic places to begin. However, the foundational wisdom from St. Benedict invites us to intentionally close the gap between sacred and secular in order to see and experience all of life—its circumstances, people, and creation—through the lens of God's constant, spiritually forming, creative Word.

His work, *The Rule of Benedict*, "is not a treatise in systematic theology. Its logic is the logic of daily life lived in Christ and lived well."[11] Benedict ordered spiritual formation and all aspects of community life within his Rule. Most often contemporary culture rebels against rules. With the perspective of self-made people in the Western world, there is little room for regulations from others. Benedict's Rule for spiritual direction is more of a guide than a hard-and-fast set of regulations. Does that mean it is optional? No. All the monks followed this guide into a single-minded focus on God for life.

Benedict encourages disciples to single-mindedness through the Rule by encouraging interior listening. Interior listening is foundational to three-way listening. With the "inner ear" of our heart we are deeply formed by the Word of God, which influences our actions, interactions, silent pauses, and reception of others. The results of Benedict's Rule practiced daily by individuals and collectively in community is that the community is transfigured into even greater Christlikeness. For a contemporary sample to develop a personal Rule of Life around the tools of spiritual direction training, please see Appendix A.

One foundational spiritual discipline from *The Rule of St. Benedict* is gathering the community together routinely throughout the day (and sometimes the night) for collectively praying Scripture. This communal rhythm of prayer, the Daily Offices, is a powerful tool for churches to soak God's Word deep into the heart. As the Word of God seeps deeply into the disciple's heart, Scripture can be prayed through all circumstances and seasons of life. With this deep listening to God through Scripture, Benedict led monks across the divide between information and formation.

---

11   Joan Chittister, OSB. 2005. *The Rule of Benedict: Insights for the Ages.* New York: Crossroad Publishing. Page 16.

One form of praying Scripture is called *Lectio Divina*. In Latin, *lectio* means "reading," and *divina*, or divine, means "holy." This holy, formational reading of Scripture empowers God's Word to engage both heart and intellect for a deep interior shaping of the reader or hearer. While praying the Scripture, attitudes, hopes, and imagination within the hearer or reader are transfigured. This expands a more focused and holistically integrated heart and mind throughout the day.

The question of how to close the gap between secular and sacred is before us. For Benedict, praying the Scripture was not just an intellectual exercise. In contrast to the modern era of scriptural exegesis—that is, mining the text for historical or theological meaning—Benedict's intent was to open space within for God's Word to become the stabilizing foundation of life. It is gaining a new lens through which to view the world, a lens that sees God in all things. Praying Scripture in community has the potential to unify secular and sacred so that we can see and hear Christ among humanity.

With rhythmic and frequent attention given to praying Scripture, the pray-er's heart is formed more nearly into the image of God. This is the stabilizing formation that draws the pray-er nearer to God's heart no matter what life circumstance is experienced. With the tools of spiritual direction training from Benedict we may discover our own inward stability on the chaotic seas of culture.

Pause and Ponder

We conclude this section on St. Benedict with a selection from *The Rule*. His words still gift us with an image of transfiguration through which he encourages love of Christ within and through the spiritual director and directee.

Listen readily to holy reading and devote yourself often to prayer.[12]

We read, after all, that our holy Fathers, energetic as they were, did all this in a single day. Let us hope that we, lukewarm as we are, can achieve [reading all of the psalms together in community] in a whole week. . . . Let us consider, then, how we ought to behave in the presence of God and his angels and let us stand to

12 Timothy Fry, editor. 1982. *The Rule of St. Benedict in English*. Collegeville, MN: Liturgical Press. Page 28.

sing the psalms in such a way that our minds are in harmony with our voices.[13]

Clothed then with faith and the performance of good works, let us set out on this way, with the Gospel for our guide.[14]

Still your mind and heart this day. Take a few deep breaths; inhale the power and presence of God, and exhale all that is resistant and overextended within you. Once you have calmed your interior heart, ponder these questions.

- How many psalms do you read with community weekly?
- With the gospel as your guide, read the Holy Week texts, beginning with the triumphal parade on Palm Sunday and ending with the crucifixion. After reading through the chapters of Holy Week, write an informational list of each day's events during that week. Your list may include things like a parade, silence, turning over tables, betrayal, denial, arrest, crucifixion, entombment. Please list these points on the respective weekday on which each event occurred.
- Next, read the Holy Week texts for formation. Listen with the inner ear of your heart as you consider the following:
  — Which of these events have you most recently experienced? What was that like for you?
  — Which event are you most drawn to? What could God be whispering to you through this event?
  — Consider what it would be like for you to stand in Peter's position and walk beside Jesus toward crucifixion.
  — Imagine you were present at the foot of the cross for crucifixion. What was that like? How did God encourage your heart when Jesus commended his mother to the beloved disciple?
  — When you gaze on the congregation and realize people are in all these various states, how are you, the leader, called to ever-deepening compassion?

May the passion of Jesus' Holy Week anoint your life for leadership.

---

13 Fry, *Rule of St. Benedict*, 47.
14 Fry, *Rule of St. Benedict*, 16.

> The monarch chrysalis is made from the inside out. "When the final molt
> beings, the caterpillar's dangling filaments [upside down] will no longer
> be 'perky.' They will hang limp and twist in spirals. Soon the caterpillar will
> begin contracting just behind the head, the skin will split open to reveal
> the emerald green chrysalis. Contractions continue, with the old skin
> proceeding to be split and shoved up, accordion-style toward the top."
>
> Baumle, *The Monarch*, 25.

In the wild wilderness of culture, God raises up leaders. You and I have the potential to become leaders filled with the Holy Spirit and with ancient wisdom from those who have come before us. It is not new structure and programming that invigorate the heart of God's people. Together the art of spiritual direction wells up into almost unimaginable brilliance of resurrecting possibility. This is the gift Benedict insisted that all within the community partake.

St. Ignatius

On occasion our intentionality to enter more deeply into awareness of God is practically forced on us. That is what happened to St. Ignatius of Loyola. During the French and Spanish war in 1517, Ignatius was injured by cannonball fire. In his bedbound recuperation, he wanted to read romance novels. Instead, he was brought books on the saints of faith and the life of Christ. "As he read these books, his fantasies began to move in another direction. He began to imagine himself in the service of Christ the King.... By the end of his convalescence, [Ignatius] had begun to review his life and his goals. His question seemed to be 'To what is the Lord calling me?'"[15]

Ignatius' openness to God and the yearlong examination of life shifted his daily routine. Intentionally, he went to live at a monastery, where he practiced "a life of prayer, fasting, vigils and new disciplines."[16] He continued to seek examination of his imagination, the Scriptures, and his own conscious awareness of God. This practice became the foundation of his spiritual writing known as *The Spiritual Exercises*.

15 Bedolla and Totro, "Ignatian Spirituality," 172.
16 Bedolla and Totro, "Ignatian Spirituality," 172–73.

The term "spiritual exercise" denotes every way of examining one's conscience, of meditating, contemplating, of praying vocally and mentally, and other spiritual activities. . . . For just as strolling, walking, and running are exercises for the body, so "spiritual exercises" is the name given to every way of preparing and making ourselves ready to get rid of all disordered affections so that, once rid of them, one might seek and find the divine will in regard to the disposition of one's life for the salvation of the soul.[17]

The formal instruction of *The Spiritual Exercises* is one way of spiritual direction. A major part of *The Spiritual Exercises* is Daily Examen of consciousness, as in Appendix B. Like an archeologist who looks backward through artifacts of a past era, the pray-er seeks to notice how God longs to be present in our lives.

A word of clarification about this process of examen. The exercise of examen is a process of learning to gaze at one's life experiences with the eyes of God: "Self-examination is not morbid introspection or self-condemnation, but the honest, fearless confrontation of the self, and its abandonment to God in trust."[18] It is seeing beyond self-incrimination and self-aggrandizing. It is the process of noticing how God loves deeply within each heart and how God yearns to be noticed in the midst of busy agendas.

We might wonder how the Daily Examen could affect people in today's frenetic culture. Daily Examen is more than a checklist of activities. It is a way to increase conscious awareness of God's energy and presence in everyday life. Once the surprises of God are habitually noticed throughout the day, there is no going back to old ways of life and prayer. This gifts us with a new lifestyle and new actions for life. This spiritual direction training tool assists the practitioner in decreasing the dualistic mindset and striving to pray without ceasing throughout the day.[19]

---

17 Gerard W. Hughes, SJ. Translated by Michael Ivens, SJ. 2004. *The Spiritual Exercises of Saint Ignatius of Loyola.* New York: Morehouse Publishing. Page 1.

18 Marjorie J. Thompson. 1995. *Soul Feast: An Invitation to the Christian Spiritual Life.* Louisville, KY: Westminster John Knox Press. Page 86.

19 "Rejoice always, pray without ceasing, give thanks in all circumstances; for this is the will of God in Christ Jesus for you" (1 Thess 5:16–18 NRSV).

Pause and Ponder

We conclude this section on St. Ignatius with a selection from *The Spiritual Exercises*. His words still give us an image of transfiguration through which he encourages love of Christ within and through leaders.

> *Remember to make use of your examen questions each day at noontime and evening. The consistent use of the examen questions will dramatically increase the transforming power of your life. . . .*

The grace you are seeking this week *is the ability to be in awe of God.*

Reflection
- When were you wowed by the person of God today? What were the circumstances?
- What was your response? Why?
- How did that moment make you feel about God?
- If there was not a moment of being wowed by God, why do you think that was?
- What did you purpose to carry with you throughout the day?
- How successful were you in bringing that purpose to mind from time to time?
- What impact did this prayer of recollection have on you?[20]

Pause now and ponder with wisdom formation from St. Ignatius.

Still your mind and heart this day. Take a few deep breaths; inhale the power and presence of God, and exhale all that is resistant and overextended within you. Once you have calmed your interior heart, ponder these questions.

---

20   Larry Warner. 2010. *Journey with Jesus: Discovering the Spiritual Exercises of Saint Ignatius*. Downers Grove, IL: InterVarsity Press. Page 89.

Examen Questions

- When and how have you been *consciously aware* of God's presence creating, acting, comforting, loving, empowering, encouraging, and listening throughout the past six hours?
- When during these past six hours have you been *unconsciously aware* of God? Time of unconscious awareness of God is not thinking of or making any notice of God's beauty, presence, or energy.
- What will you do tomorrow that might assist you in becoming more consciously aware of God throughout your day?

May the penetrating gaze of God's love fill your heart with ever-deepening awareness of God.

With the decline of the monarchs, a form of spiritual exercise has been created to assist in saving the monarch: ". . . in 2016, the USDA's Natural Resources Conservation Services (NRCS) invested $4 million to assist farmers and ranchers in 10 states—Ohio, Indiana, Illinois, Wisconsin, Minnesota, Iowa, Missouri, Kansas, Oklahoma, and Texas—in the creation of additional monarch habitat on their property."

Baumle, *The Monarch*, 56.

In the wild wilderness of the frenetic activity of daily life, the process of transfiguration begins. This does not just mean taking time away on vacation or recharging our inner batteries; rather, masterfully, the Holy Spirit leads us through metamorphosis, leaving old understandings and emerging with new perspective through the long, loving look of spiritual direction.

Rev. John Wesley

Like Benedict and Ignatius, Wesley personally experienced the formational spiral toward union with God through good, difficult, and trying circumstances. His mother was his earliest spiritual director, alongside his father, who was ordained in the Church of England. While learning to read, the Bible was his textbook. Each assignment was discussed through formational conversations. He carried forth the methodical discipline of prayer, Scripture reading, and formational conversation into his astute reorganization of the church as an adult.

Wesley was an organizational expert for spiritual formation and direction. However, he seldom used the term *direction*, fearing that it put too much power in the hands of the spiritual guide. The spiritual guidance [Wesley] taught was called "Christian confer- ence," in which people experienced mutual spiritual guidance in classes, bands, societies, families and "twin soul" and faith mentor- ing pairs. . . . People looked to [John Wesley] for spiritual guidance for exactly the same reasons as Christians across the centuries have turned to spiritual directors.[21]

Wesley encouraged everyone, regardless of age and experience, to engage in faith-forming community and conversation. Like Benedict, Wesley believed that through praying the Scriptures, God's desire could be discerned. For both Benedict and Wesley, Scripture reading was a heart-forming discipline, not just an intellectual pursuit. Wesley instructed leaders to guide heart-sharing conversations and experiences of God in small groups.

These small groups were for edification, examination, and encourage- ment of faith formation. Like Ignatian examen, Wesley asked for a review of daily living. The focus question was, "How is it with your soul?" This was not just a routine question. One could not deflect a personal answer with theology and doctrine. Wesley firmly believed the community is formed differently when authentic experience of God's presence amid personal life is shared. To minimize temptation and maximize Christian formation, Wesley divided group participants by gender, skill, or leadership position.

Like Benedict, Wesley encouraged a Rule for Life. Wesley wrote a methodical rule for all small groups for spiritual formation. This was called the General Rule. Its focus was on inward acts of piety and outward acts of justice and mercy. His intention was that small and large groups always adhered to both inner and outer components of this General Rule. Works of mercy and acts of piety were to be lived both publicly and privately.

This *is* the process of spiritual formation as Mulholland defines it— being more nearly conformed to the image of Christ for the sake of others. It is here in the Wesleyan movement that group spiritual direction solidi- fied faith formation in community. The wonder of how small groups can be structured for spiritual direction and guidance to affect people in the

21 David G. Benner and Gary W. Moon, editors. 2004. *Spiritual Direction and the Care of Souls*. Downers Grove, IL: InterVarsity Academic. Page 118.

individualized contemporary world is vital to ponder. Often, people are hesitant to share personally and deeply with others for fear of reprisal. Fears may lead to questioning if confidence will be breached. Or perhaps someone will deem us unworthy or unfit for service. With highest ethical integrity, the foundational discipline of small-group spiritual direction can assist with diminishing fears and increasing transfiguration of congregations.

Pause and Ponder

We conclude this section on Rev. Wesley with a selection from his methodical spiritual guidance for small groups. It is here the leader blossoms from individual pursuit of spiritual formation to leading others into a heightened search for the Divine through spiritual direction.

"Wesley wrote five starter questions to be used in each band meeting. Following are these questions stated in contemporary style:

1. What spiritual failures have you experienced since our lasting meeting? What known sins, if any, have you committed?
2. What temptations have you battled this week? Where do you feel the most vulnerable right now?
3. What temptations have you been delivered from this week? Please share with us how you won the victory.
4. Has the Lord revealed anything to you about your heart and life that makes you want us to join you in taking a second look at what might be sinful attitudes, lifestyles, or motivations?
5. Is there any spiritual problem that you have never been able to talk about—to us or even to God?"[22]

Pause now and ponder wisdom formation from Rev. John Wesley.

Still your mind and heart this day. Take a few deep breaths; inhale the power and presence of God, and exhale all that is resistant and overextended within you. Once you have calmed your interior heart, ponder the first

22 Gray W. Moon and David G. Benner. 2004. *Spiritual Direction and the Care of Souls.* Downers Grove: IL: IVP Academic. Page 121.

set of questions for the individual and the second set of questions for the congregation.

For individuals:

- How frequently do you meet with a small group for faith-forming conversation? How do you meet, through teleconference, face to face in person, or on the phone?
- If you do not currently have a small group, what three or four people will you invite to join you in group spiritual direction?

For the congregation:

- What is your image of God? Consider how your image of God may affect your personal and professional leadership.
- Draw a picture of your relationship to God. What would that look like? Where is God in relation to you, the congregation, and the community at large?
- What does it feel like for you to intentionally spend extended time with God?
- What is the invitation from God that you hear?

May the Trinity gift you with a community of people excited to walk out of the old wineskins and into new God possibility.

In the wild wilderness, it is easy to be fooled into removing heart focus from God. There are copycat caterpillars and butterflies that fool us into thinking they are monarchs. "One that does look very similar to the monarch caterpillar is that of the Eastern black swallowtail. . . . There's no confusing the adult butterflies, yet in caterpillar form, it happens all the time. . . . similar colors, and both have stripes. But there are distinctive differences."

Baumle, *The Monarch*, 33.

The wild wilderness of culture occurs for each generation. Throughout time, spiritual guides hold safe, sacred space as midwives birthing new interior formation for the leaders and communities. The reality of Mulholland's definition of Christian spiritual formation is lived, as the leader is more nearly conformed to the image of Christ not for self alone, but always for the sake of others. This is seen from the wisdom-faith giants of the early *ammas* and *abbas* of the desert, from St. Benedict, St. Ignatius, and Rev. John Wesley to contemporary leaders. Ministry leadership springs from the deep well of personal experience, understanding, and articulation of God. When lifelong spiritual formation of the leader is personally pursued, it becomes the foundation for transfiguring ministerial leadership.

The leader descends toward greater union with God, moving through the three stages of spiritual awakening. Times of disorientation arise, which cause the leader to go on a heightened search for the Divine. As the leader experiences these awakened stages in faith formation, the opportunity arises to lead the congregation through a similar experience. Is this a straight line of descent? No. However, each new insight brings increased conscious awareness of God, as God slowly morphs our inward hearts. Tools of spiritual direction assist the leader on the journey through chaos toward resurrection.

Temptation abounds in our current culture. The slippery slope of ethical behavior for leaders and the general population is rampant. Bullies begin to oppress others at an early age. Distinctions of lying have been made between little white lies and bigger ones. Sometimes we become stuck in less-than-stellar pursuits. The need for great ethical care in spiritual direction is just as important now as in the day of Wesley.

The contemplative life born of silence and solitude is a must for our culture. This moves hearts and minds toward deep holy listening to seeing beyond the surface presentation of conversations, circumstances, and snap judgments of others. Together as spiritual director and discerner, the leader has the potential to leap over what has been a limiting experience or understanding, and discovers God's Third Way of love.

When Hungering Hearts Get Stuck

In the wild wilderness of our fast-paced, multitasking culture, it is easy to become stuck in habitual ways of praying, looking at life, and interacting with others. We come up with all kinds of excuses for remaining in our current ways of relating to God. If the leader is to move toward the heart of God, he or she must be able to leap over that which limits his or her growth in being more nearly conformed to the image of Christ.

In the book *The Critical Journey: Stages in the Life of Faith*, Janet Hagberg and Robert Guelich emphasize that regardless of the stage of formational life we are living, there is always possibility and potential to become stuck.[23] We may be so joy-filled and comfortable with our current experience of faith that we simply do not think about moving closer to union with God. Perhaps fears, anxiety, or doubts plague us as we venture forth. Old voices from our life's history may haunt us, insisting that we live less than our greatest potential. Without a safe and sacred person with whom to share these thoughts, feelings, and resistances, we may regress or remain stagnant in our lifelong pursuit of spiritual formation. We might even let go of faith altogether. Or we may even become skilled at stealth-like living, burying feelings of stuckness underneath a shining exterior of faith. "Another sign of stuckness is having to be right and convincing others of our rightness, at any stage in our journey. Having to be right, whether liberal, New Age, evangelical, or natural is stifling. It keeps us from being open, just as any obsession keeps us from focusing on our own role in a relationship."[24] Moving through the spiritual molting of awakening, we all get stuck at one time or another.

Unfortunately, like it or not, we often get a perk from our stuckness that entices us to remain limited in our downward formation. Maybe our stuckness provides us something to complain about. Or it could divert attention away from our own perceived shortcoming. Perhaps our stuckness appears to be the way of least resistance in difficult relationships. For whatever reason we discover ourselves stuck, God is the source of freedom and new life.

I am reminded of the episode in Matthew 14:22–33, when Jesus walked across the water to the disciples' boat in a middle-of-the-night storm. There he found the disciples stuck. They were frozen with fear, unable to imagine any other possibility. Jesus came to the disciples in their deepest place of longing. They knew that they desired to be out of the storm. They were afraid for their lives. But did they notice the hunger vying for their attention from within?

After Peter's attempt to also walk on water, he and Jesus climbed into the boat. It was then that an interior change dramatically took place in the

---

23 Janet O. Hagberg and Robert A. Guelich. 2005. *The Critical Journey: Stages in the Life of Faith*. Salem, WI: Sheffield Publishing Company.

24 Hagberg and Guelich, *The Critical Journey*, 11.

created order. The disciples experienced nature differently. They looked at one another differently. They noticed a strength within Peter beyond the presentation of self-appearance. Peter had walked on water for just a step, but it was a step nonetheless! Most important, they saw Jesus as the Incarnation of God. The power-creating Word of God provided peace during the storm. In that instance, the disciples moved through stuckness into a new stage of faith. We too move through the stages of faith throughout our lives. This spiral descent of formation moves us toward greater union with God.

Moving through the stages of stuckness and forward motion of faith inspires our love. During this faith movement we commonly experience faith-life stages inclusive of the need for forgiveness, which might lead to reconciliation, self-acceptance, and acceptance by others, which in turn leads to a place of belonging in community.

Acceptance of self as one loved and created in the image of God is paramount to loving others. By the open posture of self-love (not narcissistic, controlling love) we begin to look for and see beyond the surface indwelling of Christ in the other. As we spiral nearer the ever-loving heart of God, we move toward the unconditional love of God. This increasing Christlikeness shapes our actions, attitudes, thoughts, and motivations, and unveils our ever-deepening hunger: "We move from seeing ourselves as the center of the universe to seeing God as the center of the universe from which point we serve others."[25]

Knowing our stage of faith may lead us to greater understanding of our heart's hunger. Through a spiritual life assessment or inventory we can discover what potentially limits our leaps in faith formation and what may open us to move toward metamorphosis. An inventory of this nature combined with spiritual direction may reveal how our heart hungers could influence the lives of others.[26] Hagberg tells of her own spiritual journey.

I believe spiritual direction to be a lifelong endeavor. Its daily disciplines of prayer are teaching me to live more deeply. I am learning to let go, to be led, to forgive, to love, to wait, to sever. I have more peace, more fun, more willingness to deal with anxiety, more willingness to see myself and less fear. I feel spiritual direction and

25 Hagberg and Guelich, *The Critical Journey*, 18.
26 Hagberg's assessment tool may be found by searching online for "Spiritual Life Inventory by Janet Hagberg and Terry Donovan" or by going to www.janethagberg.com/uploads/3/9/3/4/39346357/spiritual_life_inventory_120910.pdf.

other counseling have led to deep inner healing of pain, both spiritually and emotionally, that I was not even aware of before. It transformed my early childhood religious misunderstandings into meaningful realities. I don't know where I am headed in the future, but I'm learning to be more comfortable with that ambiguity. . . . I am open to God's molding me at this point in my life.[27]

Who assists you to notice the deep hunger, stuckness, and yearnings of your heart? How could a spiritual midwife open you to even greater pliability for God's heart-molding? In the wild wilderness of our fast-paced, multitasking culture, it is easy to become comfortable in our routines. However, like the caterpillar, we are meant to live even more than currently is experienced; our outward vision for life morphs as the Third Way of Christ is lived.

The Third Way

The cascading descent through spiritual direction forms the deepest inner heart of the leader. Through his or her life experiences with routine practice of prayer disciplines, the leader incrementally—or, occasionally, instantaneously—walks out of the old wineskins. Just as the caterpillar molts, walking out of restrictive skin, no longer is the leader constricted by the threats within or beyond self. The newly Spirit-formed and Spirit-led leader embraces the Third Way of God as the foundational influence for life. Does that mean he or she has gained mastery over belief and spiritual formation? No, there is no mastery in spiritual formation. Will the leader ever make missteps once he or she has been through the metamorphic stages of awakening? Yes, we are human. As the Third Way deepens within, it becomes a consistent interior heart posture and the leader's foundational choice for life and ministry.

The Third Way, which Jesus lived, *looked* like a disaster from a human perspective. When Jesus was crucified, it must have *felt* to the disciples like all was lost. However, the Spirit-formed and Spirit-led leader, who puts the intentional prayer work in, is transfigured by God's formational metamorphosis and realizes the lie. Disorientation and the chaos of the crucifixion is not the last Word. Jesus entered the disorientation of humanity to empower us to take flight. The leader who listens with the ear of his or her heart

---

27 Hagberg and Guelich, *The Critical Journey,* 25.

becomes an embodiment of God. The incandescent light of Jesus within the leader shifts from impulsive response of flight or fight to the Third Way of Jesus' translucent love.

The Third Way moves us from centeredness on "I," "me," "us," and "them" to oneness. As attachments to relationships, things, events, thoughts, outcomes, hopes, and dreams lessen, a new God-lens perspective opens for the leader. We move through the divinely created order without the need for defensiveness, judgment, harsh words, lies, or control. We do not become less of a self but more, and we grow toward the self that God intends. With the descent of the mind into the heart, a new rhythm of life is created. This gift of new rhythm causes us to see Christ in all things. Perhaps justification of position and posture is released as collective Christlike humility rises. The leader's sole attachment is grafted into the heart of God. This forms a new response. That new response is compassion.

Compassion becomes the lens through which the Third Way of life may be lived. The word *compassion* means to suffer with. This is so much more than just a moment in time when one's heart is pierced with pity, sympathy, charity, or mercy. To suffer with another is to walk beside another, articulating that we too have the same roots of imperfection and humanity in our own lives. We join in solidarity with the other's suffering, united through the heart of Jesus' suffering.

Compassion is not about getting bogged down in feeling bad for the other's suffering; it recognizes the *Imago Dei* in the other. Compassion leads us to see the woundedness of Christ's suffering in the other. It is this incandescent expression of interior formation that bears witness to Christlikeness within humanity. Through the personal metamorphosis of God's luminous presence, the leader is ready to step up, step out, step forward, and lead the congregational caterpillar through the molting metamorphosis of awakening with increased compassion.

Is this a journey that leaders can make alone? Possibly. However, it is very easy to deceive ourselves into believing what we desire is God's best desire. Christianity is not a solo pursuit. We are called to walk alongside one another, leaning up against each other for support, clarity, accountability, discernment, and ever-increasing compassion. These are the gifts of spiritual direction.

As the leader reaches the final molting and emerges from the translucent chrysalis of inward formation, the Spirit-led and Spirit-formed leader begins to lean into the dual focus in spiritual formation: first, the intentional commitment to the leader's personal lifelong journey of metamorphosis and, second, making ourselves vulnerable to lead from the tools of spiritual direction training. The leader opens the Third Way for the congregation to take flight, sharing the tools of spiritual direction training and prayer. Entering the silent abode of God's cocoonlike womb through the tools of spiritual direction training, we too can morph into God's new creation. But before we can take flight, we turn to training the heart through tools of spiritual direction training within the church. This potentially leads to a wondrous discovery of spiritual direction's ever-deepening union with self, God, and our place in mission to all the world.

Spiritual Direction Readiness Assessment and Congregational Examen

At the end of each section is a Spiritual Direction Readiness Assessment and Congregational Examen. As mentioned earlier, consider creating a portfolio, either on the computer or with pencil and paper. Within this portfolio, record your responses to the assessment and examen. At the end of this book, review your portfolio of responses. Ponder how God is inviting you further into the metamorphosis process for leadership and within the church.

Worksheet of Assessment and Examen: How Is It with Your Soul?

Personal Leadership Assessment

A. Did you have time to access the spiritual life assessment by Hagberg? If so, what are the results? If not, where do you place yourself on the spectrum of maturity in faith?

Spectrum of Faith Maturity

1. The inward journey
   a. Just beginning—recognition of God
   b. Beginning to live as Jesus' loves
   c. Finding yourself stuck
   d. Hitting the wall
   e. Seeking beyond current experience
2. The outward journey
   a. Just beginning—recognition of God
   b. Beginning to live as Jesus' loves
   c. Finding yourself stuck
   d. Hitting the wall
   e. Seeking beyond current experience
3. How are you finding the strength and beauty of your uniquely created you?
4. What outward expression shows that you are living unconditional love of God?

Giants in Faith-Wisdom

5. What wisdom from the historic giants of faith attracts your heart? Why?
   a. *Ammas* and *abbas* with silence and solitude
   b. St. Benedict with a disciplined life without a secular and sacred divide, praying Scripture and listening with the inner ear of your heart
   c. St. Ignatius with Daily Examen of Consciousness
   d. Rev. Wesley with small-group spiritual direction

Please close your time of prayer with this or one of your own prayers.

Amazing God, One in Three and Three in One, you truly are the spiritual director and guide on this holy way. I know that where I am in this moment is right where you love me. I am so very thankful for your all-encompassing love. You lead me by the heart into new stages of faith and spiritual awakening. May I be pliable in your hands to be formed into even greater love and depths of passion for you. Thank you for expanding my imagination, opening your way before me. I seek your strength to move into the next spaces you would have me live and love. Amen.

Congregational Examen

A. Where is the congregation on its faith journey?
B. Where do you place the congregation on the spectrum of maturity in faith?

Spectrum of Faith Maturity

1. The inward journey
    a. Just beginning—recognition of God
    b. Beginning to live as Jesus' loves
    c. Finding itself stuck
    d. Hitting the wall
    e. Seeking beyond current experience
2. The outward journey
    a. Just beginning—recognition of God
    b. Beginning to live as Jesus' loves
    c. Finding itself stuck
    d. Hitting the wall
    e. Seeking beyond current experience
3. How is the congregation finding the strength and beauty of its uniquely created being?
4. What outward expression shows that the congregation is living unconditional love of God?

Giants in Faith-Wisdom

5. What wisdom from the historic giants of faith attracts the congregation's heart? Why?
    a. *Ammas* and *abbas* with silence and solitude
    b. St. Benedict with a disciplined life without a secular and sacred divide, praying Scripture and listening with the inner ear of its heart
    c. St. Ignatius with Daily Examen of Consciousness
    d. Rev. Wesley with small-group spiritual direction

Interface of Personal and Congregational Response: Stages of Awakening

- *Disorientation:* How do you and the congregation experience chaos and confusion?
- *Heightened search for God:* How have you and the congregation noticed an increased intentionality and search for God's Divine presence in the midst of leadership, mission, and everyday life? Where do you get stuck? What are your usual ways of praying?
- *Change of consciousness:* What new ways of prayer have taken hold within the congregation? How is leadership and the congregation expanding new wings of flight in prayer and mission? What is an invitation from God for moving forward into a transfiguring metamorphosis?

Please close your time of prayer with this or one of your own prayers.

Amazing God, One in Three and Three in One, you truly are the spiritual director and guide on this holy way. We know that where we are in this moment is right where you love us. We are so thankful for your all-encompassing love. You lead us by the heart into new stages of faith and spiritual awakening. May we be pliable in your hands to be formed into even greater love and depths of passion for you. Thank you for expanding our imagination, opening your way before us. We seek your strength to move into the next spaces you would have us live and love. Amen.

Three

TOOLS FOR TRAINING
THE HEART

The Chrysalis Stage of Spiritual Life

It is the job of the caterpillar to join in the process of transfiguration. It is not by the caterpillar's own effort—that is, walking out of old skin, spinning the silk, and twisting—but through an interior mysterious connection with God, the caterpillar becomes a new form of life. This Divine intersection is a subconscious act on the part of the caterpillar as it lives into the natural process of metamorphosis. The caterpillar settles into cocooning in the hiddenness of God within the chrysalis. Similarly, it is the job of the church to become a safe, sacred place for people to experience the process of becoming. But unlike the caterpillar, we have choice and God-given, grace-filled opportunities to, as Paul says in 2 Corinthians, become "a new creation" in Christ (2 Cor 5:17).

This section focuses on the collective experience of the congregation. The wonder is what it could look and live like for us to intentionally follow the Spirit-formed and Spirit-led leader into the stillness of God's transforming womb. What would happen if the congregation could release its posturing, presuppositions, and positions, and consent to the stages of metamorphosis and awakening (disorientation, heightened search, and a change of consciousness)? It is unrealistic to even hint that all the membership of a church would participate in spiritual direction. However, the *tools* of spiritual direction training have the potential to bring entire groups of believers into the transfiguring process of awakening.

As the church enters God's mysterious chrysalis of formation, consider times you have settled into expectant anticipation, consented to powers beyond your own, and waited for Divine indwelling for your life. This is not a passive waiting. It is a time of intentionality. It is a time of vulnerably consenting in openness to the inward formation of God's mysterious, transfiguring love. It is in the silence of cocooning that the consenting caterpillar is captivated by the fullness of God's power. How are we, collectively as the church, giving our full consent to God's transfiguring indwelling? What would it be like if many of us, in community, sought this descending way of transfiguration? How could the church become even more of God's incarnate love and presence, translucent for all to see God's glory?

Within this section, the tools of spiritual direction training will be explored. These tools are the same ones the individual experiences in spiritual direction; however, we will discern how the leader can utilize these tools collectively within the congregation for the metamorphic possibility of transfiguring the soul of the church.

An Overview of This Chapter

We dive straight into the heart of the matter with the foundational practice of silence from desert wisdom. Silence becomes our constant companion in spiritual direction. Through silence, an increase of self-knowledge gifts discerners within the congregation with the ability to release attachments and rightness. This opens the way for the congregation to explore how God is leading them into a new way of being, seeing, and loving self and others.

Silence creates potential for parishioners to become a non-anxious presence. A non-anxious presence doesn't feel threatened. Those trained with tools from spiritual direction do not worry about setting each other straight. God knows how best to lead people to deepened faith experiences and expressions. The non-anxious person trusts that God leads the conversation and will take the community to the perfect topics of conversation. It is this posture born from silence that is the foundation for the practices of holy listening and storytelling.

Threads of God's nourishment are woven through this section. Through noticing the interior movements of God, we honor God as we seek to see beyond the presented surface of life and discover our place of belonging. It is through this heightened search for the Divine that God's nourishment swells within the body of believers and knits our hearts together in an unshakable way based on the attributes and characteristics of Christlikeness. This provides the illumination of God's interior light to transfigure the body of Christ. When people beyond the congregation encounter parishioners in mission and within interpersonal conversations, they too notice the gentling and powerful presence of God. This transfigures the congregation into its greatest potential to become a safe, sacred place of belonging for others.

The lifelong adventure of spiritual formation is not for the faint of heart. Through each of these teachable skills and deepened experiences of God we may discover resistances within self and imposed by others. It is easy, as mentioned in section 2, to become stuck by limited beliefs, fears, doubts, and threats from others. This third section concludes with a gentle look at these resistances and some possible ways of taking flight beyond that which limits our leaps in life. It is here through these tools of spiritual direction training that the chrysalis of the church has the potential to become translucent as attachments are released and people grow into new hope.

Silence

Silence is a primary foundation for spiritual direction. Silence opens space within our personal being and congregation to notice God's Divine whisper. Silence is the fertile ground of God's formation for the birthing of new life. Just like the monarch caterpillar that hangs encased in the silence of the chrysalis, our silence too becomes the womb of God's greatest desire for our lives. Congregations must become very comfortable with silence. Sometimes there may be long pauses of silence in conversation as one listens deeply, thinks, and discerns how to respond to a question that is just asked. How does one grow comfortable with silence?

"Over the next 11–15 days, the chrysalis will be home to the developing monarch butterfly. . . . As the day of enclosure draws near, the chrysalis will begin to darken, and the faint image of wings can be seen."

Baumle, *The Monarch*, 26.

For churches to fully enter into communal silence, space must be given. During worship and fellowship gatherings, people generally flock to their friends and family in the pews. For some this creates a sense of being in community. It also has the potential to leave lone individuals with a sense of separateness from the community. How could we begin to leave space for God in the pew beside and around parishioners so that each one could feel safe enough to enter silence personally while being enveloped in the community of God's silent, nurturing womb?

The first experience of silence in community that caught my heart's attention was during my spiritual direction training. When we entered the chapel for our first experience of community silence, we were unprepared for how powerfully God was noticed. The leadership of the program gave us one instruction upon entering the prayer-soaked chapel: "You may sit anywhere you like. However, be mindful to leave a lot of space between you and the next person. We must be intentional to leave ample room for God to be among us."

To enter into silence as community we must be intentional to leave "ample space for God." Wow! What a statement. We sat scattered through-out the chapel. From that experience of silence in community—that is, being alone before God with others—my concept of community prayer morphed. Being alone together, no longer could we just sit beside one another, getting as many people as possible in the pews. From that first experience through the rest of the class, my classmates and I delighted in leaving ample space between us for God. God's presence literally swelled and enveloped each one of us separately and as an entire community.

The results of that first time sitting in silence together left our com-munity with a gentler presentation of perspective. We intentionally sought to see beyond the surface presentation of classmates. We sought to notice Christ in the other. The grip of competitiveness and individualization vying for "me first" was melted away. We were brought to the soft place of God's collective cocooning. We strove to treat each other with our greatest inten-tion to live as Jesus' loves.

When sitting alone together in the silence of God's prayer, participants have the opportunity to literally become vulnerable before God within our own silent prayer. Time seems to stand still as we pray. We may even for-get that we are sitting with others in the room who are also descending their own prayer path into the heart of God's stillness. As everyone gives full attention to God, not distracted by a fidgeting pew neighbor, the silence of God's heart penetrates each person's heart. Those of us in community rest in God through our own prayers with openness and vulnerability. It is into this posture of being alone together in the silence of community that the thickness of God swells within the community and knits our hearts together as we descend the spiral of God's formative presence in silence, even though we do not share one spoken word.

The congregation that rests in silence together experiences a gentling of spirit when others are encountered. Gifts of being alone together in God's silence are born from the reality that we become a non-anxious presence. Concern about fixing others or setting them straight is lessened. Compassion becomes the lived mark of community. Before we explore the next tool from spiritual direction training, becoming a non-anxious presence, let's examine some of the challenges to collective silence.

Challenges to Collective Silence

Consistently over the past thirty-plus years of my ministry, within the local church and most recently in teaching at the seminary, I have noticed silence gets push-back from participants. Silence is very countercultural. Background noise is present in almost every venue of life, from elevator music to the white noise of the television running unattended in the background. Parker Palmer, author and wisdom leader, in his book *A Hidden Wholeness: The Journey Toward an Undivided Life*, has a prelude titled "The Blizzard of the World." He opens with lines from a Leonard Cohen song by the same title.

> The blizzard of the world
> Has crossed the threshold

Parker continues:

> There was a time when farmers on the Great Plains, at the first sign of a blizzard, would run a rope from the back door to the barn. They all knew stories of people who had wandered off and been frozen to death, having lost sight of home in a whiteout while still in their own backyards.
>
> Today we live in a blizzard of another sort. It swirls around us as economic injustice, ecological ruin, physical and spiritual violence, and their inevitable outcome, war.[1]

With all the injustice and unrest swirling throughout the world and thoughts jumping around in our minds, is silence even an option?

---

1   Parker Palmer. 2004. *A Hidden Wholeness: The Journey Toward an Undivided Life.* San Francisco: Jossey-Bass. Page 1.

Silence has received a bad reputation within many circles of humanity. Can you imagine that some people use silence to manipulate and control other people? Some people have fallen into the trap of using silence as a response when they really do not want to do the tougher, more truthful work of speaking tough love, offering different perspectives, critiquing, or offering guidance. Within the settings of churches, families, and individual relationships, there are times when people are silenced—that is, when individuals are not able to speak their truth. This gag order is detrimental to all involved. The one silenced does not have the opportunity to state their experience or share their knowledge of what is being discussed. However, the one doing the silencing is also in a less-than-healthy position. By not allowing others to speak through intimidation tactics, powering up and over another person, or by prejudgment and bullying, the misuse of silence to prohibit the other to speak diminishes all persons, self included.

Additionally, extended silence may give the practitioner too much time to think, remember, and feel through traumatic or unpleasant memories. These people expend a lot of energy trying to push down memories, and they find silence a threat to their masked, undealt-with feelings. These misuses of silence are very prevalent in our society and church. Misuses of silence leave many people personally leery of silence within the spiritual direction relationship and of becoming vulnerable before others in silent prayer. But there is hope!

Parker Palmer continues in his prelude to *A Hidden Wholeness*:

> It is easy to believe the poet's claim that "the blizzard of the world" has overturned "the order of the soul"—easy to believe that the soul—that life-giving core of the human self, with its hunger for truth and justice, love and forgiveness—has lost all power to guide our lives.
>
> ... The soul's order can never be destroyed. It may be obscured by the whiteout. We may forget, or deny, that this guidance is close at hand. And yet we are still in the soul's backyard, with chance after chance to regain our bearing.[2]

It is Spirit-formed and Spirit-led leaders and congregations that have the potential to open space within the hesitant heart by consistently engaging community in silence so people can be alone with God together. This ever-descending way toward greater union within and through God's collective

---

2   Palmer, *Hidden Wholeness*, 2.

experience of silence provides assurance that the blizzard of the world has not overturned the collective soul of the congregation.

Pause and Ponder

We conclude this section on silence with a wisdom saying from the desert. These words gift us with an image of transfiguration through the collective wisdom of silence.

> "Abba Poemen said that Abba John said that the saints are like a group of trees, each bearing different fruit but watered from the same source. The practices of one saint differ from those of another, but it is the same Spirit that works in all of them."[3]

Reflection
- How does the living water of the Holy Spirit penetrate the roots of congregational life with silence?
- What fruits of being alone together in God's silent womb of formation are lived through your congregation?
- Ministry, mission, and vision arise from the foundation of collectively shared silence. Pause and ponder how you could begin to implement the spiritual discipline of being alone together in the collective silence of community.

Pause now and ponder the practice of silence in
community, or being alone together.

Still your mind and heart this day with silence. Take a few deep breaths; inhale the power and presence of God, and exhale all that is resistant within you and that you can imagine as resistance to silence within the congregation. Once you have calmed your interior heart in silence, ponder these questions.

Examen Questions
- How will you implement silence, the foundational training tool of spiritual direction, into

---

3   Christine Valters Paintner. 2012. *Desert Fathers and Mothers: Early Christian Wisdom Sayings.* Woodstock, VT: Skylight Paths. Page 133.

    a.   leadership teams,

    b.   small group,

    c.   activities, and

    d.   the congregation at large?

- Who will assist in the planning and implementation of this intentional step into being alone together in silence?

    a.   Will those assisting you in planning be within or beyond the congregation? Is it a mixture of both?

    b.   How could a spiritual director assist in the planning and implementation of integrating silence as foundational to all aspects of congregational life?

- How will you and other leaders experience being alone together in silence?
- Does the congregation need to be educated on silence before beginning to practice? If so, how will that happen?
- How could Lenten, Advent, Pentecost, or Ordinary Time be a season of invitation for the congregation to the discipline of collective silence?
- Will parishioners practice silence at least three days a week, twenty minutes each day, at home to prepare for coming together for the collective practice of silence?
- If parishioners are practicing silence alone at home, when and how frequently are you going to invite them to come together for being alone together in silence?

May the silent union with God knit your hearts together as leader and congregation, leading you into and through the metamorphosis process of spiritual awakening. Together may you experience the luminous process of becoming.

"The larva, or caterpillar stage, lasts about 10–14 days. When the caterpillar reaches its fifth and final instar, it will be very plump, . . . It is at this point that the caterpillar will start wandering, looking for a suitable location to pupate, or form its chrysalis. Seldom does the caterpillar form its chrysalis on the milkweed plant upon which it was feeding, and it's not uncommon for a monarch to travel 40 feet away to find a place it feels provides adequate protection."

Baumle, *The Monarch*, 23.

Increasing trust, vulnerability, and openness of heart is vital to the inward transfiguring process of metamorphosis. In addition to this silent time, teaching skills for quieting the brain and focusing attentiveness is very helpful. This may come from previously mentioned styles of prayer such as mantras, centering prayer, and breath prayers. Or it may take a more active form of focus by engaging the body in movement through walking, jogging, hiking, swimming, or ballroom dancing. Creative arts prayers with coloring and contemplative photography increase silence. It does not matter how you still the jumping thoughts of the mind, but it is important to routinely mine the gem of silence.

The gem of silence illumines our belovedness. God's indwelling love shapes us incrementally more and more into Christlikeness as we learn to be still, attentive, and expectant. Through being alone together in collective silence, we become a non-anxious presence. The life-giving fruits of silence cannot be stressed enough. Patience is elongated; generosity of spirit more pronounced; removal of resistances, perceived rightness, and prejudgments of others all may be washed away with the regular rhythmic practice of silence. Through consistent practice of silence, the practitioner becomes a safe and sacred person for others to experience the presence of God. The first step of becoming a non-anxious presence is to know ourselves deeply as God's beloved even with our human imperfections.

Does the transfigured butterfly worry? Hanging upside down in the chrysalis with a completely different worldview, does it ever yearn for the former freedom of inching along the ground? Does it realize that there is no going back to the old way of life? Has it been able to release its inner self-understanding as a caterpillar and conceive that it is now God's newly formed butterfly? With this new form of life there are new ways of relating to the world. Is the butterfly awaiting final maturation within the translucent chrysalis excited with curiosity about how to move in this new way of living? Is it ready to launch into the world free of constraints as God's beloved beauty?

Leaders and congregations alike shift in interior self-understanding as they descend the silent way of metamorphosis into awakening. Congregations only can move into and through this process as far as the leader is able to immerse him- or herself into the formational process. If the leader gets hooked on something, that is often where the congregation too finds itself with limited leaps for ministry transfiguration. We digress from the congregational perspective of this section to highlight the importance of the leader knowing him- or herself—bumps, warts, imperfections, and all—as God's beloved.

Know Thyself (Leadership/Congregation)

Leadership

The question before the leader is, Have you done the interior work to know yourself? That knowing consists of acknowledging what an amazing creation of God you are! It also highlights what limits your leaps in faith within community and interpersonal skills. It has been said that each one of us has at least three personae: the person we think we are, the person others experience us to be, and the person we actually are. Unfortunately, these three personae can be very different. The goal for the Spirit-formed and Spirit-led person is to have these three personae as close in nature and presentation of self as possible.

The Spirit-formed and Spirit-led leader knows how to be intentional in his or her response rather than react with the flight or fight impulse. There are many ways we may achieve this deep inner self-knowledge. Some find intuitive formation through readings, conversations, and prayer. Often, we need a differing perspective from spiritual directors, coaches, pastoral counselors, therapists, or psychologists. The result is what is important. By coming to know our personal history and gaining the ability to live from greatest emotional, spiritual, and mental health as God's beloved, the professional side of the leader becomes equipped personally to lead a congregation.

The late Father Henri Nouwen published volumes of books on the inner spiritual journey from brokenness to healing. His book *The Wounded Healer* bears witness to the power of inner healing. The subtitle of that book tells it all: "In our own woundedness, we can become a source of life for others."[4] That is the power of knowing yourself. Historic feelings, incidents, and words no longer have ultimate sway over the Spirit-led and Spirit-formed individual. He or she walks with courage through his or her best leadership, mishaps, and imperfections to live from his or her truest identity as deeply loved by God.

---

4   Henri J. M. Nouwen. 1990. *The Wounded Healer: In Our Own Woundedness, We Can Become a Source of Life for Others.* New York: Doubleday.

The authenticity of this person becomes transparent. The theology of the Passion story of Jesus' disorientation, death, entombment, and resurrection becomes for leaders a lived experience as they traverse their personal history. People can see Christlikeness through the leader who has done the difficult work to discern how Jesus is present through personal disorientation and chaos, which leads to a heightened search and gifts the leader with a change of consciousness.

Through the midwifery ministry of spiritual direction, this courageous leader learns even greater skill in articulation of the metamorphic process. This is the leader who is vulnerable, strong, courageous, and clear enough in heart and mind to walk the congregation soulfully into their belovedness. This is the leader who can cultivate a feeling of trustworthiness from the congregation as parishioners work to claim their truest identity as God's beloved ones.

Congregation

The congregation contains a mixture of all types of personalities, abilities, and communication styles, with varying degrees of mental, spiritual, relational, and physical health. Yet even with all these variables, the importance for parishioners to know themselves as beloved of God is vital. Congregations also have three personae: the one they think they present to the public, the one they really are, and the persona of how others experience them to be. The closer in nature and action these three personae are for the soul of the congregation, the more beautiful and authentically ready it is to take flight as God's beloved in mission and to receive others in community.

One of the foundational tasks for congregational awareness of knowing thyself comes from Nouwen. I no longer remember where I read this, but its imprint stayed with me. Nouwen states that what is most personal is most universal. All people have fears, hungers, thirsts, jealousies, loves, moments of greatness, and moments of less-than-greatness. Each one experiences these inward realities of feelings and consciousness. Life circumstances may differ, but our humanity remains.

We are, however, unique in our experience of the same feelings. One may find that a storm is so scary they hide under the covers. Another may think the storm is awesome and stand on the front step watching it. However, we all have feelings and states of conscious awareness that influence our perspective. In articulating our common humanness, we find a starting point for naming our belovedness. We are imperfect, fallible creatures of God, and yet, we are God's beloved ones.

God loves us even with our imperfections and weaknesses. With God's preference for the poor, this may mean human finite ability is one of our greatest allures for God. Time and time again through years of ministry, coaching, and spiritual direction, I have companioned people through chaos, disorientation, and crises of whiteout blizzard proportions. More times than I care to count, my life has imploded with betrayal, lies from friends, system failures, and my own inward mishaps. The question becomes, How willing is the collective body of blessed misfit-believers to step through rather than around the disorientation and chaotic times of collective and individual life? Does the congregation ever fall back into the perceived security of the known and comfortable ways of deci- sion making, communication, prayer, or hierarchical stance for powering up to get agendas approved and accomplished? Has the congregation ever taken for granted their trustiest identity as a soulful church, stepping over the attributes of Jesus' character and forgetting to claim soul-deep belovedness?

Disorientation of life is often very difficult to get through. When the roadblocks of anger, pain, uncertainty, breech of ethics, scarcity of resources, theological division, "rightness," and feelings of insecurity (to name a few) arise, it may feel to the church like an impassable mountain. The congregation may fall prey to begging God to remove the barriers that are perceived roadblocks to hope and new life. Often the cry is heard from the congregation, "If only we had a different pastor, things would be better." This congregation is interested in putting blame on someone else rather than jumping into the deep end of the pool and doing the difficult community work of knowing themselves as a congregation. The congregation must wade through the chaos and disorientation to know themselves as a church that is deeply, earnestly, and solidly rooted in their soulful name, God's beloved.

Instead of going through the heart of the pain and suffering of dis- agreement, division, and sorting out the communal truth, the congrega- tion may take the bypass around pain and suffering. Some power up and demand that a certain direction is the way the church should go to avoid the struggle. Yet it is precisely in the struggle that the God-shaping for- mation of community occurs. It is through the struggle in the depths of God's silence that increased compassion is birthed. By putting in the per- sonal and collective community work of releasing attachments, knowing belovedness, and soaking in God's prayerful presence together, the church may hear the whisper of new creation dawning as a change of consciousness becomes reality.

We read of one wrestling through disorientation and fear with God in the Old Testament. After cheating Esau out of his birthright and later fleeing the wrath of his father-in-law, Jacob was poised to meet his twin brother after years of being apart. Jacob tried to appease his brother by sending presents ahead of his personal greeting. The messengers came back with word that Esau had brought a huge army with him for the reunion. Jacob recoiled in fear. The disorientation and chaos of life caught up with him. Even though he tried to be faithful, fear still filled him. That is when Jacob wrestled (Genesis 32).

In Jacob's heightened search for God, he passionately prayed (Gen 32:9–12). But fear was not dispelled by Jacob's fervent prayer. His brother and the army of men were still coming. Jacob was still thinking from his own personal perspective. He wanted to live! Jacob also thought creatively of ways to appease his brother (Gen 32:13–21). All through that night God's formational presence wrestled with him as Jacob agonized for a blessing in his own right.

> When the man saw that he did not prevail against Jacob, he struck him on the hip socket; and Jacob's hip was put out of joint as he wrestled with him. Then he said, "Let me go, for the day is breaking." But Jacob said, "I will not let you go, unless you bless me." So he said to him, "What is your name?" And he said, "Jacob." Then the man said, "You shall no longer be called Jacob, but Israel." (Gen 32:25–28a)

During the wrestling match through the silence of the night, Jacob crossed a new threshold in his life. His story moved from the individual to communal aspect of morphic awakening. The dramatic shift within his inner being gifted him with new inward strength. This was represented outwardly by a new name, Israel, which knit Jacob's heart permanently together with the community. He no longer cared just for self, but for the people of God.

As a leadership team or congregation, how willing are you to step up, into, and through a new threshold of God, no matter how fearful or illogical it may seem? Could stepping into and through a new spiritual threshold open the congregation to God-sized potential of new flight? This intentional choice of deepening trust of God even when we cannot see where, how, or when God is leading draws the congregation deeper into God's new perspective. This is an incremental collective process as the congregation moves into hope with a heightened search for God. Each time we earnestly wrestle with and open our communal self to God's interior formational shaping, the potential for God's illumination to shine a bit brighter from within is opened. It is here in going through the hurdles, resistances, and stumbling roadblocks of church that transfiguration of God's wooing, winsome lovelight illumines chaos.

Amid struggle, the congregation is transfigured more nearly into the image of Christ. This is not just for the church's sake so that people within feel part of a Christian family. This transfiguring is for the love of God and love of others. This potentially brings the congregation to a translucent place like the upside-down soon-to-be butterfly in the final days within the chrysalis, so that others beyond the church may see God's love illuminating through the congregation. As leaders accompany congregations through the rough seas of disorientation, wrestling with God through heightened search, the opportune time for deepening congregational intentionality in the spiritual life is warranted. Before we explore the next tool of spiritual direction training, the action-reflection method for deepening communal awareness and articulation of God, let's examine some of the challenges to knowing thyself as God's beloved.

The Challenge to Know Thyself

It is a difficult process to move a congregation from disorientation and the old ways of doing things into a newly deepened congregational identity. The Spirit-formed and Spirit-led leader needs agility of discernment with the various mannerisms, learning styles, personalities, and distinctive levels of mental, spiritual, and physical health within a congregation. This agile interior posture equips the leader with formational and informational ways of teaching and leading congregational experiences of formation. A challenge comes if the leader is stuck or resistant to providing a variety of expressions and experiences to spiritually equip the congregation.

Conflict within the congregation becomes another challenge to the congregation living from their truest belovedness. Conflict has the potential to sidetrack the descending movement toward deepened awakening. This moves the congregation away from formationally spiraling toward God's heart. Attention and leadership are easily diverted to mediation and conflict resolution. Conflict may easily trap a congregation in a limited identity.

Congregations divert attention from deepening their rootedness in God's identity as they profess other names for themselves. Two congregational names parishioners are especially fond of for the church are "family" and "fellowship." The challenge becomes how to deepen these two beloved attributes of church so that parishioners traverse God's spiral of formation together. Moving beyond potlucks to occasions for praying out loud together and listening with the inner ear of the heart for God's presence and guidance is very important. Becoming family beyond the cultural image of human community challenges the leader and congregation to widen their perspective to one that is inclusive of God's diverse human family. These challenges are not insurmountable. With patient, tender care and reliance on and trust of God, the strategic leader weaves formation into and through the congregation.

Pause and Ponder

We conclude this brief overview of knowing thyself as God's beloved with a wisdom saying from Father Henri Nouwen.

> It will take a great deal of time and patience to distinguish between the voice of your wounded self and the voice of God, but as you grow more and more faithful to your vocation, this will become easier. Do not despair; you are being prepared for a mission that will be hard but fruitful.[5]

Reflection
- What is the vocation of the church?
- How and when have people within your congregation raised a ruckus of disorientation to impede the descending way of God's formation?
- What have you found most helpful in sustaining the vocational call of the congregation?

Pause now and ponder the practice of knowing thyself.

Still your mind and heart this day with silence. Take a few deep breaths; inhale the power and presence of God, and exhale all that is resistant within you and that you can imagine as resistance to deeper and expanded

---

5   Henri J. M. Nouwen. 1996. *The Inner Voice of Love: A Journey Through Anguish to Freedom*. New York: Doubleday. Page 100.

congregational formation. Once you have calmed your interior heart, ponder these questions.

Examen Questions

- As leader, how have you done the difficult interior work to release old baggage and enter lightly into God's new perspective for your life?
  — What joys and resistances have you encountered within this work?
  — Who companions you on this healing way?
- For the congregation, how have parishioners done the difficult interior work to release old baggage and enter into God's metamorphic transfiguration?
  — What resistances arise?
  — Who leads the resistance?
  — How does this resistance limit leadership and congregational leaps into new possibility?
- As a congregation, how does the community claim its truest identity as God's beloved?
  — How do people beyond the community experience the congregation's belovedness?

May the gift of community and God's belovedness anoint your life this day with greatest possibility.

"The monarch does not grow in size once it has become an adult. . . .
Those caterpillars who eat less than some of their friends may form
slightly smaller chrysalides and become smaller adult butterflies."

Baumle, *The Monarch*, 19.

One intentional technique for deepening awareness of God is the action-reflection method. In congregational ministry, there are many opportunities for action-reflection. Through holy listening and inviting others to experience God and learn to speak of God's presence and power encountered through spiritual disciplines, mission, and ministry, congregants move through rather than around the heart of formation. It is not just the act of prayer and acts of mercy that shape the individuals of a congregation. The action-reflection conversation before, during, and after events, as well as worship and praying together, can lead the church toward the descending Third Way of Christ.

Action-Reflection Methodology

Many spiritual disciplines enable a community to practice action-reflection. Surrounding each activity with a pre- and post-reflection period has the potential to shift the congregational culture toward deepened spiritual formation. As previously explored for the leader in section 2, *Lectio Divina* and Daily Examen are two specific types of prayer that can be easily modified from personal use to communal action-reflection.

To pray *Lectio Divina* with groups, teams, and congregations, the questions shift from personal to communal. Along with the shift to community reflection questions, it is important for the leader to choose texts that are accessible. This means texts that are no shorter than three verses and no longer than five to ten. If the chosen verses are embedded in a longer story, the leader needs to equip the community by telling the complete story before the steps of praying Scripture.

The same text is read out loud in community four times, with a period of extended silence between each reading. Following the first reading, people have the opportunity to ask informational or clarifying questions of the text. Then deepened prayer begins. Following the silence, the community shares out loud their responses to the question. Possible questions for communal *Lectio Divina* with team leaders are directed toward their area of ministry. For example, following the second reading, the question might be, "What word or phrase best describes your ministry area from this text?" Following the third reading, the question becomes, "Where does the text intersect with your ministry area?" Following the fourth reading of the text, since we affirm that God speaks to us through all the Scripture, "What is God's invitation from the text for your ministry area?" After these four readings of the same text, the final step in community *Lectio Divina* is praying the invitation that the person on your left heard from God through the Scripture.

This final step in community *Lectio Divina* is spoken community prayer. Each participant is invited to pray another participant's invitation that was individually discerned in step four above. The instructions before the fourth reading may invite each person to write his or her invitation on a piece of paper. This may be an invitation from God for the pray-er to be or do something. For example, if reading Matthew 14:22–33, when Jesus walked on water in the midst of a raging storm, an invitation may be to step out of the boat like Peter or perhaps to trust God through the storms of life. Once the invitations are written down, each person passes his or her invitation to the person on the left. Thus, the pray-er has the neighbor's prayer invitation. After papers are exchanged, each person prays out loud his or her neighbor's invitation.

Praying another's invitation out loud has a twofold formational impact upon the church. Each pray-er steps out of his or her own desires and leans into the invitation of the other. This lessens the ownership and can move from silo configurations of ministry. Praying another's invitation from God out loud in community allows all present to hear the heart of the pray-er. In hearing others' prayers, the community is enveloped with an awareness of God's presence. It is like the practice of being alone together in silence. This opens space among the community for God to abide through the community. Toward the end of this subsection, you will hear a true congregational story of how *Lectio Divina* prayed with a leadership team expanded outreaching ministry.

Another spiritual discipline from section 2 that may be easily adapted for communal use is examen. The questions from St. Ignatius's Daily Examen shift from personal to communal as illustrated in table 1, to lead examen within the congregation.

Table 1: Congregational Action-Reflection with Examen	
Personal Examen	Congregational Examen with a Ministry Experience
1. When were you most conscious of God's presence today?	1. How did you notice God's presence during this ministry event?
2. When were you unaware of God's presence today?	2. During this time of ministry, when did you get so busy that you were unaware of God's presence?
3. What will you do differently tomorrow to be even more consciously aware of God's presence?	3. How can we plan differently our next event so that we have an even greater awareness of God?

These questions can precede or follow an event. The intention is to have the participants become attuned to listening and watching for God's presence in the midst of an activity. This also provides the community with a greater articulation of how God moves among and through them. When these dynamics are shared in community, the group itself is knit together in the heart of God differently.

Other ideas to increase congregational awareness of God's presence during activities, meetings, small groups, and teaching opportunities are illustrated in Appendix C. Appendix C highlights contemporary prayer practices of movie meditation, praying with icons, and breath prayer with walking meditation. Before we explore a final tool from spiritual direction training for morphing ministry events through asking formational questions, let's examine some of the challenges to action-reflection methodology.

Challenges to Action-Reflection Methodology

There are at least two challenges to the action-reflection method of deepening spiritual awareness and articulation of God's ever-deepening formation in congregational life. The first is slowing people down. Short of a governor's stay-at-home order, we live in an exceptionally busy time. During busyness, we church people still feel called to service; however, we prefer to serve, whether it is service projects, small groups, or fellowship activities, at our convenience. With this focus on personal time, often the volunteer for mission service calculates how long the event will be and when it will be completed. To add additional time of pre– and post–action-reflection will require that the volunteers relearn that the emphasis of mission, small group, or service is not just about doing the event, but is primarily about entering more deeply into personal and communal experience of God. This re-educational emphasis on spiritual formation rather than just doing good works for God could be a huge shift in the culture of church.

This challenge for action-reflection methodology moves the primary focus from doing to being in ministry. Acts of mercy are vital for mission. However, it is through conversational formation that we become God's love in mission. It is through increased articulation delving into our experience with God and others that we are more nearly conformed to the image of Christ. Without intentional use of formational questions through the action-reflection method, the formational piece may be omitted or left for the individual to seek out on his or her own. Or worse, the mystical interior formation goes unarticulated and is assumed to be present or falls into the cultural silence of private and personal.

How does a leader open space for the action-reflection methodology of spiritual formation to avoid this? Being in ministry challenges overly scheduled adults, families, and teens who prefer to feel productive and accomplish the task at hand. What if the leader began engaging the people in action-reflection during the mission service, small group, or fellowship time? How could shifting the friendly chatter between workers move individuals and community alike into the formational Third Way of God's love? One possible way of doing this is highlighted in the next tool from spiritual direction training: asking formational questions. Before moving to this tool, let's take an overarching excursion to look at asking questions in general.

Asking the Questions

There are different ways of asking questions. Each way of asking a question leads to a different kind of response. If one seeks factual information, asking informational or yes/no questions is helpful. These are great for clarifying information. An example of an informational question is, "What things within this book have you found most helpful?" or "Will you be sharing this book with others?"

Other questions are leading questions. That is when the asker would like the responder to answer in the manner the asker deems most appropriate. An example of a leading question is, "You have found this book very helpful, right?" These questions warrant a caution in that they mislead people or manipulate the responder into the answer that the asker would like.

The tool from spiritual direction training of asking formational questions is most helpful. These open-ended formational questions leave the responder in control of how he or she chooses to respond. Formational questions encourage the wisdom of the other to be articulated. The rules for asking formational questions are no fixing, no advising, and no setting each other straight. The responder is the expert of response to the question asked. This style of questioning honors and trusts the inward formation of God within the other. This elevates confidence in our belovedness. Just by asking the formational question, respect is shown to the responder by trusting and encouraging his or her wisdom. When used in conjunction with a ministry event, there is awesome potential to increase engagement, deepen awareness of God, and knit the community together through God's wisdom sharing.

Through formational questions, groups and entire congregations may be led into expanded awareness of God's presence amid everyday life and acknowledgment of their belovedness. A few formational questions follow.

- What was that event like for you?
- Could you say more about that?
- How could you imagine that God was present during our time?
- If you were going to draw a picture of where God was located during our event, what would that look like? What colors would you use? Where is God in relation to you in this project?

Wrapping ministry events in the context of formational questions provides the community with an openness to deepen awareness of God. Leading people in formational conversations is an opportunity of group spiritual direction, which provides the opportunity to articulate God experiences within and through community. Participants expand their perspective of how God is present within humanity as they hear one another's response.

Prior to events, the leadership has the opportunity for formational questions as well. Perhaps the leader simply reviews the questions that will be shared during or after the event. Or possibly the leader invites the community to a time of anointing prayer, which includes gifting the workers with the openness to consciously see Christ in the other. This is much more than just an opening prayer. This prayer opens the way for formational questions to be spoken before the ministry event. Questions may be asked to gift the participants with the expectation to watch for the God-energy through the experience. To provide expectation that empowers parishioners to lean into new experiences of God often brings fabulous God-sighting conversations. The action-reflection methodology deepens the collective soul of the congregation as expanded awareness of God is shared among the congregants.

Pause and Ponder

We conclude this section on action-reflection methodology with a wisdom saying from master coach J. Val Hastings's book *Change Your Questions, Change Your Church*. These words offer us an image of transfiguration through the power of questions:

"Leading with questions is a whole new leadership model. If the leadership—ordained and non-ordained—is not sold on the case for leading with questions, you will never create an environment of powerful questions."[6]

Reflection

- Imagine what it could be like to lead a congregation with powerful questions.
- How do you anticipate the culture of the congregation could shift with the use of formational questions?
- How could the transfiguring process of metamorphosis come through powerful questions?

Pause now and ponder the practice of action-reflection methodology.

Still your mind and heart this day with silence. Take a few deep breaths; inhale the power and presence of God, and exhale all that is resistant within you and that you imagine as resistance to action-reflection within the congregation. Once you have calmed your interior heart, ponder these questions.

Examen Questions

- What can you imagine would be the outcome to wrap ministry events, groups, and conversations in formational questions?
- How do formational and powerful questions have the potential to transfigure community?
- What is a possible plan for moving forward with the tools of spiritual direction training?

May the joy of experiencing God's formation through questions and prayer knit your hearts together as the soul of the congregation collectively leans into and through the metamorphic process of spiritual awakening. Together may you experience the luminous process of becoming.

---

6   J. Val Hastings. 2012. *Change Your Questions, Change Your Church.* Self-pub. Coaching4Clergy and J. Val Hastings. Page 65.

Inside the chrysalis "the monarch no longer looks like a caterpillar; in fact you will be amazed at how quickly it changed from a caterpillar to a chrysalis. How long did it take? Five minutes or so.... In about 11–15 days, depending on the temperature, it will be time for the adult butterfly to emerge."

Baumle, *The Monarch*, 116.

The trained Spirit-formed and Spirit-led leader has the learned ability and vulnerability of spirit to lead parishioners through formational practices and give strategic instructions when organizing and debriefing mission and ministry. How to ask formational questions and cultivate the dance of Divine dialogue will be explored in the subsequent subsection, "Holy Listening and Storytelling." Before we practice formational questions, it is necessary to discuss becoming a non-anxious presence.

A Non-Anxious Presence: The Release of Attachments

Do caterpillars look forward to the process of change? Do they ever want to cling to known ways of life? Just how easy is it for the caterpillar to surrender its former ways of life and fully give in to becoming a new creation in God?

Becoming a non-anxious presence lessens the human tendency to worry. The concept can be elusive in our culture. We are a people who worry. Our minds can become hooked on the imagined possibilities of what could happen. We worry because we are attached to things, people, places, and hoped-for outcomes. Attachments may be our loves, habits, theological positions, systemic structures, or routine ways of interacting with people, places, and things. We can be deeply attached to our fears, doubts, self-image, and worldview.

What does worry have to do with attachments and becoming a non-anxious presence? Attachments influence our perspective of things, feelings, people, and places. The question becomes if we love God more than the things to which we are attached.

What attachments need to be released as congregations expand awareness of their identity as beloved? Are there people that hold fast onto the past? Do parishioners in positions of administrative leadership ever cling to a position because it is the one place where they feel empowered and in control? Does fear ever grip the collective heart of the congregation as new ways for living faithfully in love of God are experienced? Living from the soulful identity of our belovedness has the potential to slowly—on occasion, sorrowfully—lead us into the process of gentling the collective spirit as attachments are released.

Through the release of attachments, patience is elongated as groups and individuals begin to look beyond the surface to notice God's presence in others. This is the transfiguring journey as change of consciousness is birthed. A shift comes in the way communities live God-presence in the world and in interpersonal relationships. This is the metamorphic process of surrender, as release of attachments occurs and the collective soul of the congregation gains deepened attachment to God.

Two Scriptures cross my mind to further understand the concept of attachments. In John 21, while sharing breakfast on the beach, the resurrected Jesus had a conversation with Peter. Three times Jesus asked Peter if Peter loved him. The conversation began, "Simon son of John, do you love me more than these?" (John 21:15b). More than what? Is Peter more attached to his feelings of denial at Jesus' arrest than his current love for Jesus? Does Peter love Jesus more than the fact that he went back to his comfortable way of life? Does Peter love Jesus more than restored relationships with his friends and family now that he is back to fishing? More than attachments to feelings, people, places, ideologies, theologies, old paradigms, familiar perspectives, and understandings of life? How much does Peter love Jesus? What was Peter attached to that kept him from being even more deeply attached to Jesus?

It is vital for believers to discern the answer to the question, More than what? What are we attached to more than our love for Jesus? Could it be family, parents, children, grandchildren, church tradition, church systems, church family, or theological beliefs and positions? If we are honest, we may find that we hold several attachments that vie for the top place of our love. How are we able to hold our attachments so lightly that they may become venues of God's opportunity for the other?

The key to formational maturation is not clinging tightly to what we love or trying to insert ourselves or God into another's world. To hold our attachments lightly gifts God with the opportunity to breathe within them and move them into deeper awareness of God, as God knows best. Learning to release our attachments is an imperative result of spiritual direction training.

As we release our stronghold on loves, fears, hopes, and dreams, we discover an ever-greater stability of heart. Please note that I use the word *stability* rather than "standing firm." Standing firm implies an inflexible stance, attitude, feeling, or motivation. Stability, for me, gives the community assurance of belovedness. As we find stability in God, we are no longer tossed by whims that come our way. Increased stability anoints the soul of the congregation with effects beyond emotional and spiritual stability of church. This soul-deep stance in the heart of God assists congregations in navigating the chaotic seas of culture. No longer will such issues as the color of paint for the sanctuary walls or the shade of carpet hold sway over people in the pews as a focal point for how to be faithful. Together, congregants experience a deepened awareness of God as attachments are released.

The second Scripture that illustrates the concept of attachment is from Matthew 14. After a long day of work, Jesus sent the disciples in a boat to cross the lake. Jesus went to a silent, solitary place to pray. After a time in the third watch of the night, a storm whipped up tumultuous winds and waves. The terrified disciples saw a figure walking on the water toward them. Once they realized it was Jesus, the challenge was set. Could Peter get out of the boat and walk toward Jesus?

Will the congregation, like Peter, do what it takes to get out of the boat? Is the congregation willing to acknowledge that we have attachments to things, people, theologies, and buildings? Is the congregation ready and willing to release attachments or worries about scarcity to grasp the hand of Jesus? Are we able to trust Jesus, living from the posture that he will sustain the church through the wind and the waves of culture, the harshest conditions of emotions, and situations of life?

It is here the tools of spiritual direction training create within us a non-anxious presence. Once we step out in trust of God, we are no longer consumed by worry and attachments. However, as with Peter, when we look squarely into the next worrisome moment or our hearts swell with great attaching love, we may falter and begin to sink into the disorienting seas. Jesus was there for Peter. Jesus is here with us. Jesus extends heart-empowering love to carry us safely to new perspectives. As we climb back into the proverbial boat, trusting in Jesus, we may non-anxiously rest in God. Like the caterpillar in the metamorphic state, this is an active rest. We are invited to become co-creators with God for the next steps of faith formation.

We become co-creators with God as congregational hurts, habits, and hang-ups, as they say in Celebrate Recovery, are transfigured into new depths of love of God.[7] This opens the way for potentially greater union of the church's three personae. Release of attachments while morphing into a non-anxious presence on the chaotic seas of culture always affects how we relate to others. It is in the depths of knowing themselves as leader and congregation that the congregation exudes belovedness. Like a luminary, or the translucent chrysalis, the love-light of God shines from within the transfiguring church for all to notice God's amazing ways of compassion, forgiveness, and redeeming love.

As the church becomes a non-anxious presence, it has the potential to be a place for all to belong. This safe space of belonging is a process. It begins with knowing thyself as God's beloved, then as community increases awareness through action-reflection methodology, deepened awareness of God and release of attachments occur. Before we move to the next training tool, holy listening and storytelling, let us look at some of the challenges for a congregation to become a non-anxious presence through release of attachments.

The Challenge of Being a Non-Anxious Presence

Culture has a deep history of clinging to attachments. The idolization of self-made persons who work themselves to death is prevalent. As financial indices fluctuate and the reality of poverty rises among humanity, oppressiveness of prejudgments and threats of violence, terror, and abuse escalate. Our attachments to things, people, and places other than God tighten their hold on communities of faith. On occasion, the love, devotion, and commitment people have to the church edifice itself border on idolatry.

With society a vast sea of chaos and disorientation, people cling to any bit of hope they can grab onto. It is a process for leadership to gain trust of congregations within this climate. Sometimes trust is elusive between congregation and leadership. Even after years of serving the church, the pastor may be seen as an outsider. Until trust is gained between leader and community, becoming a non-anxious congregation is very difficult. How is trust gained?

In becoming a non-anxious presence, as the congregation learns to surrender its listening filters and attachments, space within is opened for metamorphosis. This potentially provides others a safe community in which people can discover their place of belonging. No longer will they fear

---

7   Celebrate Recovery is a twelve-step program for recovery from addiction and for finding freedom from your hurts, hang-ups, and habits. *Life's Healing Choices*, a book by John Baker, expounds on eight of these steps for great wholeness of life.

rejection or judgment. By the congregation's open interior posture through knowing thyself as God's beloved, gentling of expression and temperament through the action-reflection method, relationship building, and release of attachments, the congregation is poised for flight.

Pause and Ponder

We conclude this section on non-anxious presence with a wisdom saying from an old Hasidic tale, "Darkness and the Dawn."

> The rabbi asked his students: "How can we determine the hour of dawn, when night ends and the day begins?"
>
> One of the rabbi's students suggested: "When from a distance you can distinguish between a dog and a sheep?"
>
> "No," was the answer of the rabbi.
>
> "It is when one can distinguish between a fig tree and a grape-vine?" asked a second student.
>
> "No," the rabbi said.
>
> "Please tell us the answer then," said the students.
>
> "It is then," said the wise teacher, "when you can look into the face of another human being and you have enough light in you to recognize your brother or your sister. Until then it is night, and darkness is still with us."[8]

Reflection

- When you gaze at another person, what is the first thing you see?
- How does the transfiguring light of Christ within gift us with eyes to see God's presence in others?
- How brightly does the light of Christ beam forth from within you?

Pause now and ponder the practice of becoming a non-anxious presence.

Still your mind and heart this day in silence. Take a few deep breaths; inhale the power and presence of God, and exhale all that is resistant within you and that you can imagine as resistance to becoming a non-anxious

---

8   Henri Nouwen, with Michael J. Christensen and Rebecca J. Laird. 2006. *Spiritual Direction: Wisdom for the Long Walk of Faith.* New York: HarperOne. Pages 109–10.

presence within the congregation. Once you have calmed your interior heart in silence, ponder these questions.

Examen Questions

- How comfortable are you with your own personal history?
- How does the congregation know its spiritual history?
    — To what hang-ups, old grudges, perceptions, and theological perspectives does the congregation cling?
- What are the resistances to metamorphosis within the congregation?
- How willing do you imagine the congregation and the leadership team are to experiment with new ways of praying with formational questions and silence?
- What is the curiosity level of the congregation?
- What is the leadership plan for wrapping ministry and meetings in formational experiences and conversations?
- What could be your part?

May you hear your name, Beloved, called throughout this day as God leads you into and through the metamorphic process of spiritual awakening. Together as leader and congregation may you experience the luminous process of becoming.

"In general, butterflies appear to have poor hearing. Larvae perceive sound through tactile setae, but they seem to mainly respond to sudden noises. This is easy to observe in monarch larvae, which will rear up if you clap loudly near them."[9]

Holy Listening and Storytelling

My curiosity led me to research if the caterpillar and emerging butterfly could hear within the chrysalis. Imagine what stories the caterpillar whispers as the metamorphic process is taking place. Does the butterfly have a different perspective? How would the caterpillar and the butterfly speak about the divine mysterious presence that gently guides it through this life-changing process?

---

9 Monarch Watch. "Sensory Systems." https://www.monarchwatch.org/biology/sense1.htm. Accessed January 27, 2020.

Storytelling and listening are powerful tools. Words express our greatest feelings of love and haunt us with feelings of fear, depression, and anxiety. Our life is a series of stories. Stories recall with whom we talked and ate, where we have been, and what we have experienced. Stories influence our world perspective. Every individual has their own historic and more recent stories. Within a gathering of people in a church, just imagine how many stories are present. These stories hold emotion and influence. Each person has his or her perspective on how the original story unfolded. What a complex story web.

The Greatest Story ever lived and told is constantly before us as we seek to live faithfully. The Bible is filled with the stories of the faithful saints and sinners of humanity as God's direct, subtle, and gentle Word whispers to the human heart. The life, ministry, and passion of Jesus the Christ is a powerful story that creates reality. The main tool for spiritual direction training is story—not the made-up kind of story or the story that harms or seeks to entrap others. Story in spiritual direction is a mixture of conscious awareness of what is happening within and through the directee's life and from beyond the conscious awareness of the storyteller. The storyteller often has an "aha" moment within the spiritual direction conversation when he or she discovers a new depth of story that reveals more of God's story within his or her life. Each story has the potential to expand awareness of God's next new thing as community spirals ever deeper through the metamorphic process of spiritual direction.

Two skills used in the storytelling of spiritual direction are holy listening and speaking the story itself. Holy listening comes from our silently stilled heart and non-anxious presence. The listener listens to both spoken and unspoken words and pays attention to tone, rate of speech, and gestures in the conversation. It is three-way listening that undergirds the spiritual direction conversation as holy listening.

There are numerous ways that people tell their story. Some drag it out. Others dramatize the story. Still others may dribble their story out in bits and pieces as the listener attempts to string the storyline together. Storytellers may go around and around the barn and never seem to get to the end of the tale. In whatever manner the story is told, it contains great potential and wisdom for deepening God's transfiguring process. There is a plethora of books written on holy listening and storytelling in and through spiritual direction. I commend them to you. Some are mentioned in the resource section of the afterword of this book.

Through the communication skills of holy listening and storytelling, greater openness to hearing God is developed. In the age of multitasking, these skills are paramount to expressing and receiving true love, compassion, and God's caring. This is foundational to congregational ministry. The way people feel heard and received is vital to the church. The two sides of storytelling are the speaker and the listener. It is important to know how the listener's own counter-story affects listening ability.

What is a counter-story? It is all the things we have been talking about thus far in this section, "Know Thyself." Holy listeners need to do their interior work of healing from any woundedness and be intentional to release attachments. Knowing thyself involves being able to separate fact from fiction in our own historical experiences and to feel very stable within self so that the listener is not swayed by the whimsical winds of life or the depth of the story told to them.

A wisdom saying from the *abbas* and *ammas* provides guidance for expanded awareness of self and God. The story instructs the seeker to look beyond the surface of life so that he or she may become even more Christlike in thought, word, and deeds.

> Another brother asked ... Abbot Theodore and began to question him and to inquire about things which he had never yet put into practice himself. The elder said to him: As yet you have not found a ship, and you have not put your baggage aboard, and you have not started to cross the seas: can you talk as if you had already arrived in that city to which you planned to go? When you have put into practice the thing you are talking about, then speak from knowledge of the thing itself![10]

I love the last line from this desert elder: "When you have put into practice the thing you are talking about, then speak from knowledge of the thing itself!" It is relatively easy to speak of things of faith, even to believe them. It is much more challenging to have these things become the only foundation for thoughts, words, and actions.

How does the gift of holy listening and storytelling become foundational for our thoughts, words, and actions? By increasing attentiveness and openness without preconceived ideas. When I first began serving as congregational pastor, we had "Listening Labs" training.[11] We practiced listen-

---

10   Thomas Merton, translator. 2004. *The Wisdom of the Desert: Sayings from the Desert Fathers of the Fourth Century.* Boston: Shambhala. Page 62.

11   John Savage and Kenneth J. Mitchell. 1979. *Lab I Skills for Calling and Caring Ministries: Learning the Language of Healing.* Pittsford, NY: L.E.A.D. Consultants, Inc. Listening Labs were presented across the West Ohio Area of The United Methodist Church in the early 1990s.

ing skills of perception checks and asking open-ended questions, discerned reasons for lack of retention within the church, and learned levels of storytelling. The levels of storytelling and listening were imprinted on my heart and mind. They are fantastic tools for spiritual direction training.

Levels of Storytelling and Holy Listening

Active listening skills involve all the senses of the listener. The listener uses sight to notice body language. (Although body language can be a confusing indicator of the intent of the speaker. Not all persons come from the same cultural perspective; an open posture in one culture may seem insignificant, misleading, or even detrimental in another culture.) The listener uses hearing for the speed of speech and the tone of voice; listening with our physical ears for spoken words leads to powerful heart-listening for unspoken words. Assumptions cannot be made about unspoken—even spoken—words. Simply holding the words before God opens the way for new insights.

Clarifying questions and statements for the speaker to articulate what he or she means by a comment or word used in the conversation is also important. For example, the speaker and listener could be in the same storm and experience it very differently. Think for a moment about the worst storm you have ever been through. In spiritual direction the vagueness of this question is intentional. Is it a physical storm (tornado, blizzard, earthquake)? Or perhaps the worst storm of your life is a crisis of relationship, job loss, illness, or devastating grief from the loss of a loved one.

For an example, let's look at the blizzard of 1978 in Ohio. One may have found the blizzard a nice reprieve from the hectic pace of life. This person may have hunkered down by the fireside heat with the sunlight by day and candlelight by night to enjoy the interruption of scheduled time to relax at home. Another may have found themselves chipping frozen peanut butter out of the jar trying to find something to eat, as lethargy set in from the cold without a working fireplace. We cannot assume because the weather event was the same that the individual experiences were the same. Holy listening requires an openness and release of judgment to be able to receive the other in his or her experience without our own story getting in the way of our hearing. Active listening opens us to receive the other at whatever level of storytelling the other shares.

Every storyteller moves through various levels in his or her story. My notes from the Savage Listening Labs depict these levels of story below.

Figure 3. Speaker's Levels of Storytelling[12]

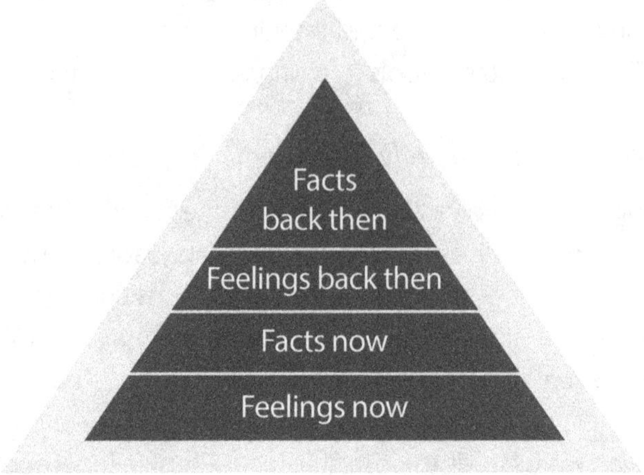

Facts Back Then are when one speaks about how he or she experienced what happened historically. This is the emotionally safest level of storytelling in that little, if any, emotion is expressed. The facts are historic events, but even more importantly, they are the way the events are personally remembered. Collectively, within the congregation, these facts are the foundation for how an event, interpersonal conversation, or circumstance is remembered. Congregations can become stuck in a story. I know of a congregation that, twenty years after an event, was still talking about the time a celebrity came to speak against an unpopular war.

If I were to tell the facts of the blizzard of 1978, they would include that the wind whipped so long and so hard through the night that drifts of snow reached as high as the rooftops of two-story homes. There were widespread electrical power outages; roads were impassable. This resulted in the city and county using front-end loaders to slowly clear the streets by scooping away the snow and lifting it into awaiting dump trucks. It was cold. To stay warm, alternative heating mechanisms were used. However, not all homes had alternative forms of heat. Those with alternative heat and those without alternative heat had differing feelings about the facts. The electricity was out for at least four days. These facts could be verified by other persons who experienced the blizzard in the same geographic area.

---

12 Kenneth J. Mitchell and John S. Savage. 1979. "L.E.A.D. Consultants, Inc. Lab I Skills for Calling and Caring Ministries: Learning the Language of Healing." Pittsford, NY: Leadership, Education, and Development. From personal notes.

Feelings Back Then, the next level of storytelling when descending the pyramid in figure 3, slightly increases the intimacy of storytelling but is still a relatively safe perspective for the one telling the story. This is where individual experiences may begin to differ. The storyteller is not currently engaged in the historic emotions but rather makes statements of facts that include how he or she felt during that time. The exception is if the undealt-with emotion still captures the storyteller's heart.

Returning to the example of the blizzard of 1978, I was cozy in my in-town apartment. The gas oven brought warmth to the tiny space. When I phoned my mother and sister living in the country only five miles out of town, I learned that their story was very different. At first, when I checked on them via phone, they were upbeat, and all was fine; they were ready to ride the cold storm out. By the fourth day, as my family endured no heat and no water, and the only food was frozen peanut butter they chipped out of the jar, my feelings kicked into another level. I began to take charge. I felt a responsibility to get them out of their home and get them thawed out. As depicted in this illustration of storytelling, at the Feelings Back Then level the listener is drawn deeper into the story as the listener's emotions engage.

The third level of active listening is Facts Now. This level moves the story from the past into the present. With this shift, the intimacy level of the story once again moves to a deeper level. As the storyteller shares the facts about what is happening within her or his life now, the listener is engaged on an even deeper level. And yet the listener is not anxious about the facts or feelings presented. It is the other's story, not the listener's story. At times, clarifying questions are helpful to assist in the telling of the story. However, this informational style of listening keeps the story at one level and does not move the storyteller to the final level of storytelling.

An example of the Facts Now listening level is not pertinent to the blizzard of 1978. (Unless you are reading this book in the midst of a blizzard now!) For an example of Facts Now, I digress a bit to catch you up on the moment of now. Several years ago (Facts Back Then), I discerned a new and shifting call from God. Serving as congregational pastor was great; however, my heart was ignited with a passion for spiritual direction (Feelings Back Then). Since that time, I have been appointed by my bishop to the spiritual formation ministry of Living Streams Flowing Water (Facts Now). I love this ministry (Feelings Now). I have so many opportunities to engage individuals, congregations, students, and the institutional church (Facts Now). Each venue of ministry is a new adventure for me in God's shared presence (Feelings Now). I am so humbled to walk beside amazing people, congregational leadership teams, and congregations that are seeking a deepened and expanded awareness of God in personal and communal life. My heart leaps with thanksgiving to God as clients' personal and professional leadership shifts to the next level. It is such a holy place of work (Facts Now and Feelings Now).

Did you notice the movement of the levels of storytelling in the above example? The descent from Facts Back Then may be a straight shot into intimacy. However, we often go up and down the levels of storytelling very naturally as we tell our story. The listener assists the storyteller by asking formational questions. Formational questions are vital to the art of storytelling and holy listening. They move the story into levels the storyteller may not have yet explored. From the blizzard story, a listener could ask the storyteller how God was experienced back then. The listener could then raise the question if the storyteller has ever experienced God in similar ways since that time. This could potentially deepen the level of conversation while moving the story from past to present.

The interesting thing about holy listening and storytelling is that the listener also has a story. This is called our counter-story. It is depicted as an upside-down triangle in the storytelling levels.

Figure 4. Listener's Counter-Story[13]

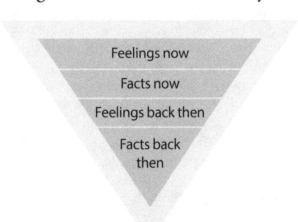

13 Mitchell and Savage. "L.E.A.D. Consultants, Inc. Lab I Skills for Calling and Caring Ministries: Learning the Language of Healing."

Are we aware of our own story? Can the congregation articulate the spiritual footprints and various levels of their communal story? Do we get stuck in certain levels? Do we avoid the depth of intimacy required in sharing our feelings now? In the collective conversation of the church, do we avoid issues in conversation so that others will not become upset? In the example of the congregation continuing to bring up the celebrity speaker, the first time I heard the story, another congregant rolled his eyes and stated, "Oh no, here we go again."

Figure 5. Three-Way Listening of Spiritual Direction

God

Storyteller's
Story

Facts back then

Feelings back then

Facts now

Feelings now

Listener's
Story

Feelings now

Facts now

Feelings back then

Facts back then

Storyteller   Listener

The healthier a person's interior posture, the easier it is for us to truly listen to others. Are we selective of the stories we share? The answer is, on occasion, yes. The Spirit-formed and Spirit-led leader seeks to increase trust among the congregation. As trust is increased collectively, the congregation may desire to gain a heightened search for God, deepening or shifting their God-wisdom stories. This can open the way for the church to slowly, incrementally, and intentionally move through the metamorphic process toward God's greatest desire for that community of believers.

The study, learning, and repeated practice of the construct of conversations is fascinating. It is delightful to notice how God becomes the true guide for listening and receiving the story of others. When we place the skill of three-way listening over the communication levels of storytelling, a powerful tool of spiritual direction training comes alive. Figure 5 depicts the triangular conversation undergirding the storytelling and listening levels.

The listener must be so comfortable with his or her own story that he or she does not interrupt the one sharing a story. In this dance of dialogue, the listener follows the storyteller's lead regardless of the level of storytelling with which they are speaking. The role of the spiritual director, or holy listener within the congregation, is to deepen and expand awareness of God in the circumstances of the story and within the storyteller's life. Questions such as "Could you say more about that?" are very transforming for parishioners. As previously mentioned, the listener must be very comfortable with silence while the other processes new God insights during the conversation. This shared presence of God during three-way listening conversations is the essence of the art of spiritual direction.

As the listener with a trained heart learns to release personal, historical, and current attachments and not interject his or her own story into someone else's story, the listener lives a stance of a non-anxious presence. This offers heart hospitality to others. This safe interior attitude gifts others with a sense of welcome, belonging, and feeling respectfully received. The listener remembers the hard-and-fast rules of no fixing, no advising, no setting each other straight, and no telling. It is not the place for the spiritual director to correct someone's theology or perceptions. The roles of teacher, preacher, counselor, friend, and mentor may breach this rule on occasion, but holy listeners in spiritual direction do not.

Formational questions that move the conversation toward the descending Third Way of God's love are open-ended questions that honor and value the risen Christ within the other. This can increase within the storyteller trust of inner wisdom, as one created in the image of Christ. The spiritual director and those equipped to use the tools from spiritual direction training are the openhearted midwives for the transfiguring process of awakening to the new insights God longs to live through each community and individual person. To learn this skill, we must turn to the key distinctions between informational and formational questions.

Keys to Informational and Formational Questions

Informational questions are the what, when, where, who, and how questions asked by journalists. These questions clarify Facts Back Then and Facts Now. This is necessary in all conversations so that the listener knows what subject is being talked about. Informational questions may be yes-or-no response questions, which if used exclusively can ultimately stifle the conversation.

If we turn to our faith journey, informational questions might include, "What is your life verse from the Bible?" "Do you believe in miracles?" "Have you ever experienced a miracle at the power and desire of God?" "Where are you on the theological spectrum?" "What Scriptures support your position?" Remaining on an informational level of conversation often leads to argumentation and difference of opinion. Each opinion is left up to the believer to defend, support, and critique. Information can leave communities reeling to justify their theological position. This may lead to deep division within the institutional Body of Christ, the Church. The Church, since the Reformation split with Catholicism, now comprises many denominations, often from fractures over informational articulation of what happens during the sacraments of the Eucharist and baptism. Most recently, the informational argument facing the Church has been over inclusion. The divisive informational questions—"Who is in?" "Who is out?" "Who can be ordained?"—have wreaked havoc on individuals and communities alike. With persistent and exclusive use over many years, information-only questions do more harm than help for deepening spiritual formation.

Formational questions are those questions to which no one knows the answer, except the responder. These questions touch the levels of storytelling that move into deepening intimacy and emotion. Formational questions may also be based on who, what, and how. This is where confusion often sets in. Parishioners may think they are asking a formational question, when they are really staying on the surface of information.

Formational questions might be something like, "How does your life verse influence your daily activities?" "Tell me about a time when you experienced the miracle of God's guiding presence in your life." "What was that like for you?" "When you encounter a person whose beliefs are very different than yours, what is that like for you?" Or possibly, when discerning between two good options for next steps, the question may be asked, "Tell me about who you are and your imagined shifts in relationship with God if you choose either option?" The use of sanctified imagination is a great technique for formational questions. An example of this might be, "If there were no restrictions and anything was possible, how do you imagine that God was present in the facts of the situation?"

Did you notice that I used the term *sanctified imagination*? Imagination is an awesome way of co-creating with God's new possibilities. Through prayer and God's blessing of our imagination, God is the one expanding our imagination. Without this prayer of blessing for our imaginations, it may become difficult to notice when we just have a good idea or if it is God's expanded imagination in our creativity and thoughts. Further, for some, the fear of the evil one absconding with the imagination is very real. By placing our imagination under the care of God's blessing, an assurance of peace might come to those who fear being led astray through the imagination. Sanctified imagination and formational questions as well as open-ended statements are the core of spiritual formation and a teachable foundational tool from spiritual direction training.

The complexity of holy listening and storytelling is experienced through three-way listening, the storytelling levels, the type of questions asked, and our counter-story. Each of these skills for deepened listening is teachable. With the added comfort of silence and welcoming hospitality of heart, the attentive focus of holy listening gifts the storyteller with a sacred, safe place for sharing dimensions of the inward experience of God. Before we explore the expansion of spiritual direction training tools for use in groups and the corporate setting of congregation, let's examine some of the challenges to collective holy listening and storytelling.

Challenges to Holy Listening and Storytelling

Many challenges can interfere with the process and opportunity for holy listening and storytelling. For example, attachments may be a huge deterrent to one's listening ability. If the listener already has a preconceived notion of how the story should or could have occurred, this will hinder the storytelling and the listener's ability to receive the fullness of the other. However, storytelling might assist in moving the speakers and listeners beyond stuckness of preconceived ideas. For this to happen, the listener must be an experienced active listener. The listener must know his- or herself so that his or her story does not get in the way of hearing the others.

It is crucial to ask formational questions. However, the challenge comes first in discerning if parishioners even want to learn and practice asking questions and attentive listening. It takes time to teach, informationally and formationally, and practice these tools with leadership, teams, and parishioners at large. Implementation of the tools from spiritual direction is a slow process of God's interior formation within each heart. Once most people learn and practice these listening skills, the church may move more freely into new experiences of formation.

Pause and Ponder

We conclude this section on holy listening and storytelling with a wisdom saying from Thomas Merton, the twentieth-century Trappist monk from the Abbey of Gethsemani in Kentucky.

> "The whole purpose of spiritual direction is to penetrate beneath the surface of a man's [or woman's] life, to get beyond the façade of conventional gestures and attitudes which he [or she] presents to the world, and to bring out his [or her] inner spiritual freedom, his [or her] inmost truth, which is what we call the likeness of Christ in his [or her] soul."[14]

Reflection
- What façades have you noticed in self and others within the congregation?
- How do you move people beyond only seeing and/or presenting a surface-level façade into soul depths of knowing?
- How does this awaken Christlikeness within community?

Pause now and ponder the practice of holy listening and storytelling.

Still your mind and heart this day with silence. Take a few deep breaths; inhale the power and presence of God and exhale all that is resistant within you and that you can imagine as resistance to holy listening and storytelling within the congregation. Once you have calmed your interior heart in silence, ponder these questions.

Examen Questions
- What is your most comfortable level of storytelling and story listening?

---

14 Thomas Merton. 1975. *Spiritual Direction and Meditation and What Is Contemplation?* Wheat Hampstead, UK: Anthony Clarke Books. Page 17.

- Does your counter-story ever get in your listening way?
- How can you imagine teaching the levels of storytelling and listening to leadership teams, small groups, and the congregation at large?
- What steps will you implement to integrate the power of storytelling and holy listening within the congregation?

May the silent union with God knit your hearts together as Spirit-formed and Spirit-led leader and congregation while you experiment with listening and storytelling. Through this practice may God lead you collectively into and through the metamorphosis process of spiritual awakening. Together may you experience the luminous process of becoming even more Christ-like in outward expression.

Migrating monarchs do not go it alone. "Migration begins in the farthest north part of their range, in the southern part of Canada, starting about mid-August. Moving in a southern and southwesterly direction, the majority of the monarchs travel through the heart of the eastern part of the U.S."

Baumle, *The Monarch*, 39.

We pause to notice the nuances of listening and seeing beyond the presented facts of life to discover what it is to gaze with the soft eyes of God. As we sharpen our listening ability, the goal becomes to notice the living presence of Christ indwelling the other. This moves our vision beyond surface judgments of accent, ethnicity, age, educational level, and lifestyle as we take a long, loving look at the other, seeing the beauty of the Divine fabric of God's presence indwelling humanity. As communication and listening skills are enhanced through heart-training with tools of spiritual direction, the practitioner begins the expansion of compassion.

With increased compassion, we are able to view others through the lens of Divine love. This seismic shift from seeing others from our own counter-story perspective to receiving others opens the way for transfiguration. The metamorphosis of relating to others on social issues and faith concerns may occur as we interact more on a formational level than just informational. These skills may be woven into the tapestry of the congregation through personal, communal, and corporate conversations of spiritual direction.

A Place of Belonging: Individual, Group, and Corporate Spiritual Direction

It is a picture to behold.

> There is no other more ready community than congregation to lis-
> ten intently for the voice of God, seek seriously for God's way, and
> faithfully respond to God's awakening call.
>   Congregational life is intended to be the fertile soil in the which
> spiritual life is born, blossoms, and bears fruit. Congregational life is
> the best place to support individuals and families in their spiritual
> journey. Congregational life is where people learn what it means
> to follow Christ and to live the Christian life. Congregational life
> is where love for God, love for self, and love for neighbor can be
> learned, practiced, and incorporated into daily living.[15]

Wow! What a picture of a congregation. This speaks to the metamorphic shift that is possible within the congregation. When the Spirit-formed
and Spirit-led leader and congregation collaboratively consent and commit
to deepening and expanding conscious awareness of God in and through
the community, the possibility of transfiguring illumination blossoms. Congregations have the potential to become Incarnational communities as
tools from spiritual direction training ground all aspects of life within the
congregation.

In implementing the tools from spiritual direction training throughout
the congregation, people feel a sense of belonging. Parishioners and leader,
together, are invited to break out of the traditional one-on-one spiritual
direction and move into community configurations for training the heart.
With the interjection of formational questions through holy listening and
the action-reflection method, each conversation can serve as spiritual direction. Creating time in agendas for leadership teams, small ministry groups,
administration, and fellowship to include faith-forming conversations is a
priority for morphing a church. With so many various groups, how can this
be accomplished?

---

15 Rueben P. Job. 1997. *Spiritual Life in the Congregation: A Guide for Retreats.* Nashville,
    TN: Upper Room Books. Page 25.

Group Spiritual Direction

It is amazing to me that the fourth-generation butterfly, the migrating monarch generation, is physically different. Their wings are slightly larger, and they lack a hormone that stimulates reproductive behavior. Yet to those of us who casually glance at the monarch, we are unable to make any distinction between the generations.

"Adult monarchs that migrate have been shown to have wings that are slightly larger than those butterflies that only live 2–6 weeks and do not migrate. The forewings especially may also appear to be darker, indicating that the scales are more densely positioned on them. Both of these factors assist the migrating monarch in its long journey."

Baumle, *The Monarch*, 38.

The tools of spiritual direction training are the same whether individuals meet one on one or in small groups, or even when used in the corporate setting of the worshiping congregation. Spiritual direction in whatever configuration it is shared within community is still spiritual direction.

Informally, spiritual direction may happen in congregations at any given moment—in hallway conversations, over coffee, on visitations to hospitals or those who are homebound, within general conversation, and even in worship. Just imagine how moving a conversation to beyond the surface understanding could ignite transformation. This necessitates that leaders and parishioners be equipped with the tools of spiritual direction training so that they can bring holy listening, formational questions, and action-reflection methodology to any given conversation, small group, and even preaching events.

Formal group spiritual direction may be used within the congregation for discernment of vision, mission, and implementation of ministry. Three resources are noted. The resources are Clearness Committee, Circles of Trust, and group spiritual direction.[16] The rhythm of group direction written

---

16 For a resource to further examine the Quaker tradition of Clearness Committee, see: Patricia Loring. 1992. *Spiritual Discernment: The Context and Goal of Clearness Committees*. Wallingford, PA: Penndel Hill Publications. Circles of Trust are a small-group process where participants learn to listen intently to the "inner teacher" of oneself. See the website for the Center of Courage and Renewal: http://www

about by Rose Mary Dougherty is one of silence, questioning, response, and listening. The focus person shares his or her presenting issue. Clarifying informational questions may be asked if needed. The presentation and any subsequent clarifying questions are followed by spacious silence for reflection of the listeners and the speaker. Then opportunity is given for formational questions. Following each question there is silence for prayer and reflection. When the formational questions have been exhausted for one focus person, that person's time of discernment is complete. The same format is followed for each participant. Silence is held between each group member's turn as speaker. Dougherty writes, "In group spiritual direction people learn to listen to God's Spirit at work in them for others in the group. . . . There is a collective wisdom available for each person."[17]

Dougherty outlines "three conditions essential to the life of the group. Members must agree to commit themselves to 1) an honest relationship with God; 2) wholehearted participation in the group process through prayerful listening and response; and 3) opening their spiritual journeys to the consideration of others."[18] It is essential to foster an atmosphere of trust within the group. The depth of sharing in formal group spiritual direction is God centered.

In a less formal approach to group spiritual direction, reflection on how spiritual formation could become foundational to all church ministry is pertinent. Through the molting process of expanding informational learning with the depth of formational experience, the potential exists for all meetings, prayer and study small groups, and service projects to be transformed into opportunities for ever-deepening articulation of God's activity within the greater community.

This is a huge shift from the traditional manner of following committee agendas. For the trained heart from spiritual direction, leaders of the business meeting realize that the top priority of ministry is spiritual formation in all circumstances within the church and that the business agenda comes second. This is a *huge* shift in living ministry. That is, the tasks for ministry are secondary to the primary focus of expanding and deepening relationship with God. Why? First and foremost, we are called to live as lovers of God.

.couragerenewal.org/. You may also refer to Palmer, *A Hidden Wholeness*. Lastly, see Rose Mary Dougherty, S.S.N.D. 1995. *Group Spiritual Direction: Community for Discernment*. New York: Paulist Press.

17 Dougherty, *Group Spiritual Direction*, 36.
18 Dougherty, *Group Spiritual Direction*, 37.

Each time community gathers, the intent of faith sharing is paramount. We love God by serving on the finance committee, acting as trustees, working on the education team, or leading worship; however, when we come together akin to the Wesleyan movement of formation, we are to care for, look after, and encourage ever-deepening articulation and awareness of God in personal and communal life. This makes using the tools from spiritual direction training vital for committees, small groups, and fellowship gathering to focus.

This shift in focus moves the community from the perfunctory opening and closing prayers of meetings to training people to lean into examination of consciousness in all situations. How does this shift occur? Through open hearts to God's spiritually forming energy among us. With an intentional examen, meetings, fellowship gatherings, rehearsals, and study and prayer groups can focus to become the womb of God's mysterious process of metamorphosis. It will amaze the group that once formation is the primary focus of the group, the business gets accomplished in record time.

Using the tools from spiritual direction training mentioned thus far in this section moves the meeting from our control and getting the tasks accomplished, to releasing ourselves to the direction and intent of what God desires for the committee. With this intentional shift, the question arises: How could all small-group and interpersonal encounters lead the way for God to expand the metamorphosis of church? Before we turn the umbrella upside down with corporate spiritual direction, let's examine some challenges that arise when forming all meetings and groups within the congregation as spiritually forming community.

The Challenge of Group Spiritual Direction

We as people like to get things done. It is no different with our faith. We like to feel productive and accomplished in whatever task we commit to. Inverting the priority of meetings to formation first and business second is very uncomfortable for many people. The first challenge is how to transition the meeting to formation first.

Which comes first, the monarch or the egg? Do we begin with the small-group experience first to focus on using tools of spiritual direction, or does the corporate focus of leading the large group of believers into deepened and expanded awareness of God come first? Or could it be necessary to invert both at the same time? You are the expert of your congregation. I offer a word of caution, however, for just beginning with small groups.

It is very easy for small-group formational experiences to fall into the programmatic arena of church. Using the tools from spiritual direction for the transfiguration of a congregation does not happen as one ministry alongside other ministries. The tools of spiritual direction training are the foundation of all ministry. If spiritual direction is strictly delegated to small groups, the congregational perspective easily can become that those groups are only for touchy-feely people and those who want to have an emotional experience of God. This emphasis is very detrimental in that it limits the potential of God's seismic transfiguration within the congregation. Just as the monarch cannot emerge from the caterpillar without a metamorphic transfiguration, neither can small groups as just one more program cause a foundational shift in church culture. This sets up a dualism that is to be avoided within congregations.

That dualism is the separation of the sacred and secular dynamics of ministry. The dualistic mindset accents that separation, that business meetings (secular) are for business and formational (sacred) kinds of ministry are for forming the inward nature of people. The assumption becomes of formational groups, "that worship is the only formational ministry needed." Often it becomes an unspoken hierarchy of which is most important. After all, we do need finances to run the church. However, the Body of Christ is founded on formation, not finance. My wonder is, Could there be anything within the church that has even greater potential to transfigure this divided mindset?

To potentially overcome these challenges, we can implement the tools of spiritual direction training with *Lectio Divina*, examen, action-reflection, storytelling, and holy listening. These tools provide formational questions to create a sacred safe space within the heart of the community. Have you noticed that I always put together the words *safe* and *sacred* when speaking of the hospitality of heart to receive others? I use both words because in reality safety cannot be guaranteed for another although it is the ideal. For some, speaking of a particular injustice such as abuse, racism, and poverty may not be safe, but it can be sacred. We can make the conversation as sacred as possibility, which in turn might make it a safe space for the other.

Pause and Ponder

We conclude this section on group spiritual direction with a wisdom saying from Bishop Rueben Job. These words gift us with an image of transfiguring congregational life through the tools of spiritual direction training:

"Spiritual life can and should be nurtured in every contact with the congregation. The building, worship, meetings, fellowship, teachings, hospitality, communication, leadership, and every aspect of congregational life should be providing opportunity for new birth, nurture, and growth in our spiritual lives."[19]

Reflection

- Review the congregation you participate in most frequently.
- How do you see spiritual formation and tools of spiritual direction training as a priority of the leadership and, subsequently, of the congregation?
  — What fruits do you see or could you imagine?
- When did you last experience a "new birth" moment of spiritual growth through your congregation?

Pause now and ponder the practice of group spiritual direction.

Still your mind and heart this day with silence. Take a few deep breaths; inhale the power and presence of God, and exhale all that is resistant within you and that you can imagine as resistant to group spiritual direction within the congregation. Once you have calmed your interior heart in silence, ponder these questions.

Examen Questions

- Review this section and consider a plan of implementation for group spiritual direction within your congregation.
- Will you design a formal process of group spiritual direction?
- What action could informally shift the prayer culture and expand attentiveness to God's Spirit for the congregation?
- What will be your intentional plan for integrating tools of spiritual direction training into groups, committees, and teams within your church?
- Who will assist you in implementation of first steps?

May these steps lead the congregation to even greater potential for the integration of these tools in group spiritual direction. Together through

---

19   Job, *Spiritual Life in the Congregation*, 26.

the metamorphosis process may your congregation experience spiritual awakening.

"When the time is right, you may notice a tiny bit of air space has formed between the butterfly and the cuticle of the chrysalis. Next, the outer part of the chrysalis will crack and you'll see the monarch pushing."

Baumle, *The Monarch*, 116.

The incremental shift in congregational culture can be very slow. Like the caterpillar at the beginning of its life, inch by inch new vision, wisdom, and articulation of God is lived, shared, and birthed among community. From individual spiritual direction to weaving tools of spiritual direction into all dynamics of church, we find the enclosure of the spiritual formation umbrella becoming cramped. This positions the congregation to be ready to spring into corporate spiritual direction. Together leader and congregation discover the umbrella of spiritual formation is ready to be turned upside down. This opens the way for God's transfiguring metamorphosis in the corporate connection of church.

Turning the Umbrella Upside Down

Metamorphosis turns the caterpillar inside out and upside down. Tools from spiritual direction training can do the same for the congregation. If small-group spiritual direction is relegated to a side programmatic ministry of the church, the full potential of using the tools of spiritual direction training within the congregation goes unmet. Like the question about the monarch—which is first, the egg or the butterfly?—the question for the church is this: Which is first, small-group or corporate spiritual direction training?

The aim is for the community at large to know inwardly the sweetness of God's infilling Spirit. Yes, individuals and small groups may be part of this igniting Holy Spirit fire. However, unless established as the foundation for metamorphosis, the congregation may lack zeal in transfiguration. God's reorientation and formation through corporate spiritual direction in the largest context of congregational ministry is necessary.

The image of an umbrella was used earlier to illustrate the overarching ministry of spiritual formation and the many practices of ministry under it to incarnate God's formation within and beyond the church. To review figure 1, please go to page 14.

Figure 6 depicts the extension of ministry through corporate spiritual direction.

Figure 6. The Upside-Down Umbrella
Tools of Spiritual Direction Training as the Basis for Congregational Spiritual Formation

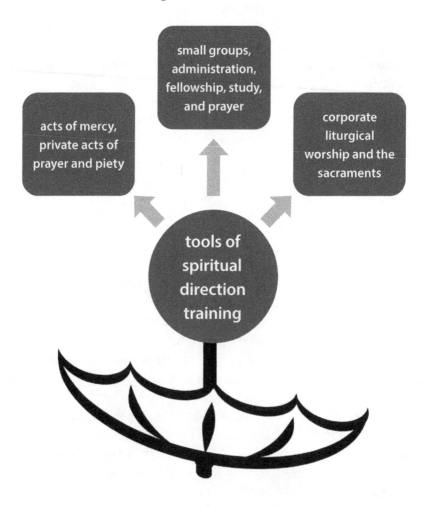

Corporate Spiritual Direction

There is at least one constant for the life of the caterpillar turned upside down within the chrysalis: the breath of God. Both forms of life, the caterpillar and the butterfly, breathe. This infilling of God's energy sustains them through the transfiguring process of metamorphosis. The question becomes, How are congregations led collectively to breathe deeply of the transfiguring breath of God in their innermost essence?

"Caterpillars and adult butterflies both breathe through tiny pores called spiracles. From each spiracle, the blue tubes, called trachea, carry oxygen into the chrysalis. . . . The insect's air lumen . . . functions like lungs in concert with the tracheae."[20]

Corporate spiritual direction is a collective experience of individuals breathing deeply of God's inward forming energy. The soul of the congregation can collectively descend nearer to the heart of God, with awakened hunger and consent to this formational process. With this, a metamorphic shift within church life is possible. For the church, breathing space into worship is of utmost importance. I wonder what limited worship celebrations to a three-point sermon, the sacraments, Scripture reading, prayers, and songs?

The intent of all dynamics of worship is to breathe in God. But how intentional are we to leave space for God among community, like the aforementioned community silence experience during my spiritual direction training? Worship is one primary event that might be shaped differently for the formation of community. Adding silence, giving full attention to threshold crossing as people transition from one aspect of worship to another, and sinking deeply into God's felt experience of worship are all possibilities.

The powerful tool of silence is not just for individuals. The wonder is how to assist congregants in becoming more comfortable with silence. Since people learn and experience God in so many differing ways, it will be necessary to provide both information and formation to increase the comfort level of parishioners with silence.

---

20 Lisa Raffensperger. 2013. "See Inside a Chrysalis as It Develops into a Butterfly." www
    .discovermagazine.com/planet-earth/see-inside-a-chrysalis-as-it-develops-into-a
    -butterfly-video. Accessed February 7, 2020.

Informationally, a simple Google search provides many scientific, humorous, and religious reasons why silence is beneficial to individuals and communities. When it comes to experiencing silence in the corporate setting, explanation either before or after the experience assists people in knowing why it is important to elongate the corporate time of being alone together in silence.

Here are a few formational ideas for incorporating more silence into worship. Reading Scripture might become an opportunity for community *Lectio Divina*. The leader could either experience *Lectio Divina* with all four readings at one time, or the *Lectio Divina* experience could be the thread of nourishment woven throughout the entire worship experience. To introduce *Lectio Divina* at the Scripture reading time, the worship leader could instruct the listeners as follows: "I am going to read the Scripture three times. After each reading, there will be a pause for silence. Following this first reading, please consider what word or phrase catches your attention. In the silence, be with that word or phrase. Let it become God's Word on your heart." Following the second reading ask, "How does the Scripture intersect with your life or ministry area?" For the third reading ask, "What is the invitation you hear from God through this Scripture personally or for your area of ministry?" When the invitation of God is discerned from the Scripture, the leader could have parishioners write their words and thoughts down on a sticky note during the reflection time. After praying the Scripture in this manner several times, the congregation may even be ready for the final prayer of blessing, exchanging the invitation that each heard with a pew partner for prayer. It may take a while to build up to using all of these questions in the worship experience. This could become a yearlong teaching tool of spiritual direction in the corporate worship to expand practice and comfort with silence.

If the leader chooses to weave *Lectio Divina* throughout the worship service, it could look something like this. After leading the people across the threshold into worship, the worship celebration begins with the Scripture reading. After the first reading, question, and silent reflection, the leader moves to song, prayer, or spoken word, then returns back to the same Scripture reading with an introduction to the second *Lectio Divina* question. Following the second silent reflection time, again, the leader could have a song, prayer, or spoken word. The leader then moves to the third reading, question, and silent reflection with the same Scripture. The leader invites parishioners to write their reflections down on sticky notes so that they can take their prayer words home with them. The use of sticky notes sets the congregation and leadership up to introduce an at-home practice of centering prayer or mantra prayers with the words heard from the Scripture during worship.

Corporate *Lectio Divina* can be used with movie clips, drama, and music. These practices transfigure *Lectio Divina* (Divine Reading) into *Visio Divina* (Divine Seeing). If the leader chooses to use *Visio Divina* in either of the above formats, it is important to keep the video clip or dramatization to two to three minutes. This assists the pray-ers in retention of the material. With music as the focus for *Lectio Divina*, the practice becomes *Audio Divina* (Divine Listening). Worship leaders may become as creative as the congregation will permit with *Audio Divina*. Perhaps the leader provides paper and pencil for creating a depiction of the music in prayerful reflection. The congregation may be invited into the meditative movement of a hand dance with *Audio Divina*.

Meditative movement with a hand dance invites people to close their eyes and simply move their hands in the tempo and temperament of the music. This expression breaks two socially accepted barriers. The first is movement: pietistic cultures do not typically move during worship. The second is silence. Please see Appendix C for further information about these tools.

Breathing space into worship can also be effective during times of prayer. Intentionally pausing in silence before speaking the pastoral prayer provides an opportunity for people to center themselves. Leading the prayer with centering sentences assists people in feeling a united presence of prayer shared among them. Prayer sentences may assist people in thinking about how God has been present within their lives during the week; this can open the way for an examen during the prayer. Examen of consciousness can be useful beyond prayer times in worship.

Examen may be used during and after pieces of worship. It could be the reflective pause after a song, highlighting the question, "How did the persons of the congregation notice God's presence during that song?" One fantastic use of examen is with the Lord's Prayer. Asking the question before each petition of the Lord's Prayer, "How have you been faithful with this petition?," is very impactful for community. Take, for example, the petition "Give us this day our daily bread." The question might be how each one within the congregation or the church itself has been totally reliant on God for provision, protection, nourishment, or things needed for healthy living. The petition "Lead us not into temptation" may provide the opportunity for people to examen the question, "Since the community has last gathered,

how and when have we been tempted?" This slowing down of the rote reci-
tation of the Lord's Prayer breathes God's presence among the community.
The Beatitudes or the Fruits of the Spirit are other great foci for congregational examen.

Providing ways for reflective, silent pause during and after the sermon
are effective. One pastor creates weekly "Lifenotes" for the people to take
home as a prayer discipline. Lifenotes are filled with thoughtful reflections
or prayer tools as an extension of the sermon to engage people at home.
Lifenotes may invite parishioners to practice a prayer technique that was
just experienced in worship. Once the foundation of spiritual direction training is built within a congregation, each month new prayer practices and
tools from spiritual direction training can be experienced by the congregation. Thus, a teaching method from spiritual direction during the sermon is
to lead the people in an experience of prayer when speaking about prayer.
This constant repetitive prayer practice provides parishioners with the
learned art to notice and speak of the interior movement of God.

There are many interior movements of God during worship. A threshold
is moving from one aspect of worship to another. Scripture reading, the
offering, songs, the sermon, and prayers are all aspects of worship that provide threshold crossing. These become vital portals for descending nearer
the heart of God. Even at the beginning of worship, when people come
rushing in from their daily routines, a threshold opportunity occurs.

When people come from home they might be rushed with little children, assisting elderly parents, driving a long way, or simply distracted and
not yet focused on God. How the worship leader invites the people to transition from the routine pace of their life to the worship event can serve as
a spiritual direction moment. The words, invitations, and music that assist
parishioners in crossing the threshold during worship are vital. This is not a
static invitation, remaining the same from week to week. The Word of God
is creative. Worship leaders are invited to be creative also. Through spiritual
direction training, the worship leader learns deep hospitality for the soul as
the leader guides people across threshold moments.

With tools of spiritual direction training, the worship event has the
potential to become retreatlike during the one-hour celebration. The
parishioners sink into God's presence as God seeps into each heart. Beyond
what has been mentioned, how can this be done? Possibly using a prayer
refrain song throughout the worship experience such as "Water, River, Spirit,

Grace."[21] Prayer songs that soak into the heart, similar to Taizé songs, are helpful to deeply infuse the heart of community.[22] Another option is using a prayer verse such as the sevenfold Alleluia and changing the words on each verse to something like "Come, Lord Jesus" or "Thank you, Jesus." Such songs may lead the congregation deeper into conscious awareness of God within and among the community.[23]

"Every species of butterfly has specific host plants on which they raise their young. Many have a number of acceptable host plants, but the monarch utilizes only one group of plants: milkweeds. Part of the reason is that these plants contain a characteristic milky latex sap, giving them their common name." The church's host plant, nourishing soul of the congregations, is intentionally being more nearly conformed to the image of Christ.

Baumle, *The Monarch*, 67.

Worship is just one way that tools of spiritual direction training can enliven corporate Christian formation. Discerning mission through prayer is a vital aspect of implementation of spiritual direction training into practical ministry. Let's pause here to consider a true congregational story of mission birthed from the tools of spiritual direction training.

It was a small church, according to the membership book. However, its members were courageous enough to follow God's Spirit-empowerment into astounding mission. Using the tools of silence, shared prayer, and *Lectio Divina*, the leadership team leaned into God's new adventure. The metamorphosis of the congregation was outstanding. By consistently praying Scripture with *Lectio Divina* for six months with the leadership team, a new outreaching mission to the community was birthed. Within the first year of this mission, more than 10,000 people were embraced with Christ's love.

---

21 Hoyt L. Hickman, general editor. 2000. *Faith We Sing, Pew Edition*. Nashville, TN: Abingdon Press. 2242.

22 Taizé songs can be found through IGA Publications at www.giamusic.com/sacred_music/resourcepage_taize.cfm. Accessed January 30, 2020.

23 Rueben P. Job, chair of the Hymnal Revision Committee. 1989. *The United Methodist Hymnal: Alleluia*. Nashville, TN: The United Methodist Publishing House, 186.

Here is our leadership story and the unfolding miracle of God's prayer lived in action as I first wrote about it in Dwight Judy's book *A Quiet Pentecost: Inviting the Spirit into Congregational Life*.

> Opening the Bible for prayerful soaking in the Word, I posed questions to the leadership team based on the historical practice of *lectio divina*. In choosing scriptures . . . , I work from the perspective that to be vital, the congregation . . . must seek the presence of God's Holy Spirit. . . . I began with a healing story so they could picture God desiring healing for them. Later, I used the scripture of Jesus walking on water and asking Peter to step out of the boat to develop their capacity for acting on faith. The final scripture was the Pentecost story from Acts 2. . . .
>
> I explained the final step in this community process of praying the scriptures. . . . I asked them to pray for one another and the invitations each had heard in the scripture. . . . As we audibly prayed the other's invitation, no one could insist "my way is the best way" or "I have the perfect direction from God." Each listened to the other's heart's desire and cared for the other's invitation to bear fruit. In that instant God began binding prayer-filled hearts together. New community was born. . . .
>
> Our discernment journey continued as we prayed scriptures out loud and set aside personal agendas at each church council meeting for six months. Then, with a unanimous uplifting of the Spirit, a collective aha! birthed new vision and life into the fragile congregation. . . . Each person was certain it was a direction from God, clearly the fruit from our practice of *lectio divina*. Unity and excitement were the marks of the Spirit's leading. . . .
>
> Prayer and mission in this congregation have transformed life in the neighborhood and in the church. A gentle-spirited seventy-year-old woman sums up the miraculous power of praying the scripture for discernment and mission. Her words still ring in my heart: "Why hasn't any pastor ever before in all my years of going here taught us to pray like this?"[24]

It is imperative that spiritual direction training include instruction for how to implement the skills learned into the local ministry setting. The goal

24 Dwight Judy. 2013. *A Quiet Pentecost: Inviting the Spirit into Congregational Life*. Nashville, TN: Upper Room Books. Pages 50–51.

is that ministry leaders create missional opportunities from a place of deep rest and discernment. This is one way that spiritual direction can assist the leadership team in planning and implementing steps for God-vision mission to come to life.

From the very beginning of ministry, Wendy Miller states, there is a need to "build apprenticeships which could translate [tools of spiritual direction training] into home congregations." Every element of ministry becomes an opportunity to "notice how Jesus comes to you, and how you respond to Jesus. That is the invitation of spiritual direction."[25] Through spiritual direction training, people begin to have softer eyes, gazing upon others and the world with the eyes and heart of God. It is here in the heart of sharing God's presence alone together that individuals and families alike find a place of belonging. It is truly lovely to belong together in God. And yet if this is so lovely, why is it not prevalent in our contemporary way of relating to others in faith? Resistance happens to deep soul work on many levels. Before we explore the resistance from within and beyond self to the tools of spiritual direction training, let's examine some of the challenges to corporate spiritual direction.

The Challenge to Corporate Spiritual Direction

"We have never done it this way before!" That cry is the challenge to implementing tools from spiritual direction training into corporate spiritual direction. Have we become habitual in the ways of worship? Is faith a private thing only, one that we keep strictly to ourselves? Any acceptance of minimal or nominal faith depth is a huge challenge to corporate spiritual direction.

Since the hope is that new people are always coming to the congregation, an open posture of prayer and adventure is needed. These seekers bring a perspective of church worship. This in and of itself may limit the expansion of corporate spiritual direction within a congregation if people come from the model of worship that is less steeped in formational practices. This leads to the challenge of corporate spiritual direction to always be teaching informationally the new paradigm of worship infused with corporate spiritual direction. The pause of many in-person worship celebrations during the time of the pandemic made this is an opportune time and occasion for doing worship differently and to increase formation through the tools of spiritual direction. The more and more congregations engage

25 Buckwell, *Rediscovering the Contemplative Tradition*, 164.

in corporate spiritual direction, the more and more potential there is for a metamorphic shift in the way we live church.

Moving from mastery of faith to the beginner's mind perspective is a constant challenge to corporate spiritual direction. Because people live and work in a society steeped in empathic mastery of skills, the beginner's mind is often elusive for people of faith. The beginner's mind does not lower one's self-esteem but recognizes that there is always so much more of God to learn and experience in our corporate and personal descent toward the heart of God. With these resistances, we wonder, Shall we talk ourselves out of striving to incorporate spiritual direction within the congregation? I trust that God is stronger than what looks like insurmountable mountains. It is in our greatest weakness, when we strive to be faithful even when things look so challenging, that God opens the way for possibility.

Resistances Within and Beyond

Resistance to spiritual direction happens. Whether it is personally challenging for an individual to remain silent, look within, or find a rhythm of coming before God, or whether it is interpersonally challenging among clergy, staff, and parishioners, the ugly side of resistance shows itself. Systemically, in the institutional church there has been resistance to deepening awareness of God's new birthing among humanity since the time of Jesus. The leaders of the ancient religious communities, the Pharisees and Sadducees, sought to entrap Jesus. This is particularly evident throughout the Gospels as Jesus made his way to Jerusalem. Even the Epistles show that some committed Christ followers were enticed toward false prophets who diluted acts of discipleship. Often others sought an easier road than obedience to God. Others were stoned to death, or were excommunicated from the Jewish temple for following Jesus. However, time and time again God triumphs over resistance. That does not mean the life journey was without peril. Remember it is through the struggle, wrestling with God, that we are most inwardly formed into God's greater Christlikeness.

The wonder for contemporary culture is if false prophets could still be present. The slippery slope of ethics is easily encountered. Does the chaos of disorientation lend itself to defensiveness of persons, institutions, and theological persuasion? Could it be a result of nominal Christianity or the busyness of schedules that causes resistance? Is it that people do not feel they have time enough to invest in a deepened search for the Divine? Is resistance experienced because generations of leadership have assumed spirituality? (Remember the seventy-year-old parishioner discussed earlier who, after experiencing *Lectio Divina*, asked, "Why hasn't any pastor ever before in all my years of going here taught us to pray like this?") Have we, the church, become stuck in the informational way of teaching because it is intellectually stimulating and easier to teach and measure concrete faith facts?

We humans are more than just head people and thinking beings. As the sixteenth-century mystic St. Teresa of Ávila proclaimed, "Christ has no body now but yours. No hands, no feet on earth but yours. Yours are the eyes through which he looks compassion on this world. Yours are the feet with which he walks to do good. Yours are the hands through which he blesses all the world. Yours are the hands, yours are the feet, yours are the eyes, you are his body. Christ has no body now on earth but yours."[26] If I may humbly suggest a possible addition to the wisdom of St. Teresa: Christ has no heart but ours to be shaped more and more nearly into the image of Christ's love for the sake of others. Through the mystery of God's metamorphosis, believers can truly experience congregational change of consciousness.

It is this metamorphic process of transfiguring leaders and communities that incites resistance. The cry as heard in the earlier section of this book, "Tale of Transfiguration," can be heard as people exclaim: "I did not know it would be *so* different than I expected." "We have never done it that way before." "Please don't rock the proverbial boat. This is my only place of security." "My church is my family. Do not mess with it." "We know what the best way is; just do it my way!" Or resistance comes in subtle, subversive ways. Rumors spread quickly throughout the church grapevine. Embellishments happen, papers go missing, we become legislative rather than compassion oriented. Perhaps resistance is shown as leaders power up and over the tops of others. Some slam hands on desks, disregard the work of others, or work to circumvent the slow descent toward inward formation.

"There has been a 90% decline in the monarch population over the last 20 years. A drop in number as severe as that begs for some explanation as to why. Has there been some environmental change that makes the monarch's world more hostile to it? And if so, what happened? Is it something that is naturally occurring or is it something that we as humans have done? The answer is both."

Baumle, *The Monarch*, 45.

---

26 https://www.goodreads.com/quotes/66880-christ-has-no-body-now-but-yours
-no-hands-no. Accessed November 11, 2019.

Resistance to God's new interior shaping comes in many sneaky ways. In our inability to decide, there is resistance. If we are struggling with our relationship with God, we may also avoid looking realistically within ourselves to see what God may be inviting us to. Some signs of resistance are avoiding prayer, falling asleep when trying to pray, being constantly "fine" (the acronym FINE is "feelings inside not expressed"), not having time to pray, questioning if God really cares or hears our prayers, and ultimately finding prayer boring and unproductive. Here are a few stories of resistance experienced within the church when Spirit-formed and Spirit-led leaders attempted to lead the congregation into the formational way of greater Christlikeness.

Resistance among clergy colleagues in ministry is prevalent. This happens peer to peer as jealousy opens the way for the gossip lines to light up with juicy tidbits. "Tradition! Tradition!" That is the cry of the senior pastor with whom Glenna (not her real name) works. He does not understand spiritual direction, and a spiritual formation stance for ministry seems like gibberish to him. "He is not open to it. He doesn't understand the labyrinth.[27] He wants ministry to be just like it was when he graduated seminary in the 1970s. I am finding that a bit hard." This senior pastor had just begun working at the church, and Glenna was hopeful that she had established a strong formational community that would assist her in working with this rigid senior pastor.

Glenna said, "He just is not open to spiritual formation for himself. . . . He comes to things that the spiritual formation team prepares, but is he there for support or to undermine the ministry?" One example of the senior pastor's intentional lack of support was seen on the Epiphany Prayer Day. Glenna had worked hard preparing for this. "There were many prayer centers, and the labyrinth was there. The senior pastor came. He sat down and took out the hymnal and read it all day. He didn't look at anything. He didn't try anything. He is very closed to it all." How is Glenna to deal with this

---

27 A labyrinth, whose origins go back to antiquity, is a maze-like pattern that one walks and is a metaphor for the spiritual journey. According to Dr. Lauren Artress, "The labyrinth can be a tremendous help in quieting the mind, because the body is moving. Movement takes away the excess charge of psychic energy that disturbs our efforts to quiet our thought processes. . . . In Western Christianity the mystical path is traditionally called the Threefold Path. The three stages that define the sequence, the process [with which] we experience an ever-deepening sense of union with the Divine, are Purgation, Illumination, and Union." Lauren Artress. 1995. *Walking a Sacred Path.* New York: The Berkley Publishing Group. Pages 25, 28.

blatant resistance to the ministry she does and still maintain collegial relations with her senior pastor?

"Clueless." That is how Juliet (not her real name) describes her senior pastor.

> For some clergy this [spiritual direction] doesn't speak at all to them. I am sure it is true for some laity also. . . . Our senior pastor is growing the church by leaps and bounds, and we have done everything on leadership. It is just making me want to climb the tree with my fingernails. But he doesn't have a clue. [This is not soul-deep growth.] He is a great guy, but spiritual direction to him is an anomaly that he won't ever grasp. And when I talk about it, he gets glazed over in his eye and doesn't listen. . . .
>
> I do not speak a lot about spiritual direction to the senior pastor; rather than to annoy him I just let it lie. There are three other elders on staff—all men, and none of them are interested in this. . . . I think they have learned a lot from the coping journey that I have been through the last few years. I planted the seeds; God will make them grow in the right time.[28]

Causes of Resistance

What causes such passionate resistance? There are two major reasons. One underlying cause is perceived loss of control. Somewhere along life's journey many of us have unconsciously assumed that we are in control. That presumed control of life extends to our own lives as we try to make informed decisions, seek to feel like life is manageable, and try to handle everything by ourselves. Our illusion of control may also extend to the lives of others. This often happens with those nearest and dearest to our hearts. At times we try to form children into our own image and make little "mini me's." Others power up with violence in an attempt to have people conform to "my best way." Still others use silence as manipulation, driving people in and out of relationships as resistance, jealousies, and insecurities are lived. Loss of control over things, people, and circumstances leaves us fearful and heightens resistance. If the one in control does not maintain the control, then what is left? A lack of trust in self, God, and others causes fear, which is then controlled through resistance.

---

28 Buckwell, *Rediscovering the Contemplative Tradition*, 101–2.

The other underlying concern that causes resistance is feeling vulnerable. If we are a generation that likes to feel in charge, then the other side of that is that we really do not like to feel out of control and vulnerable. Feeling vulnerable is an issue of power. This may come from feeling disempowered within relationships, organizations, and systemic institutions. Even when one oversees something, feelings of vulnerability can arise when she or he is threatened by the perceived power of the others. The tools of spiritual direction always bring to the forefront God's power. This in turn causes some people to rear up in resistance, feeling a threat to their position of power. Resistance is natural and should be expected.

Culturally, why is there so much resistance? What causes feelings of vulnerability and the need for control? Life is pressurized. Whether one is a pew person or a person of leadership, life is filled with demands. There are schedules to be kept, relationships requiring attention, and often overextended work hours. This personal level of pressure can easily slip into a constant threat within community. There is a feeling of great angst and protest in our worldwide culture. The nightly news incites fear as a constant commentary on the terrors of the world; pandemic, national unrest, and violence blares on the screen. This underlying systemic fear has too many people feeling the need to protect themselves with weapons. As a result of mass shootings, schoolchildren and preschoolers practice intruder drills. These protective measures may be necessary. However, in their wake, children and adults alike have a flame of fear below the surface of presented life.

Fear within faith is very real. Look at the story of Jonah. He fled God's call so long and hard that he ended up being thrown over the side of a ship in a storm. Leaders and parishioners may hold resistance to deepening his or her spiritual awareness of God just as Jonah did. The wonder is, Why are we not honored, excited, and willing to be obedient and of service to God? The worry may cross the mind and heart, "What if God wants me to do something that simply sounds too difficult for me?" I hear story after story from seminarians who say that they have come to the end of their running away from God. Attending seminary is one of the ways they are finally willing to say yes to their call. I remember years ago my own run from God's call and crying out to God, "You want me to do *what?* Who am I to do that?"

Why the resistance to God's calling, if we trust in God's goodness for us and for our communities? Do we believe the words from Jeremiah 29:11? The prophet says to weary people: "For surely I know the plans I have for you, says the Lord, plans for your welfare and not for harm, to give you a future with hope." Yet when God invites us to something new, we are often resistant.

Instead of leaning into this trustworthy God, a longing may rise from within for things to go back to the comfortable and known ways of experiencing relationship with God. Often security is sought in what is known.

Within an institution or congregation, resistance to God's deepening new prayer and spiritual direction is seen as leaders focus on increased organizational structure rather than moving together back to the basis of spiritual formation and prayer. Organizationally, this is a tricky thing. People are still praying. They are still seeking God, but it is like before and after Pentecost, which is how Jesus led the disciples into deeper understanding and an internal awareness of God's indwelling within their lives. Rupert (name changed) says:

> We are living the same struggle with Jesus and the disciples of the first century. First, they had the language but didn't have the heart language and the Holy Spirit had to come. If the Holy Spirit had not been there what would have happened to the inner life? Something beyond using words of God—a parrot can repeat words—something beyond emotional response. It is going back and recapturing what Jesus did with the disciples. When the disciples first began to understand Jesus, they understood from the outside, yet when their ministry transformed *The Book of Acts* it was very different.[29]

How does the Holy Spirit assist us in dealing with resistance to deepened awareness, interior transfiguration, and the metamorphosis of the church? There are at least three proven, effective ways.

First, we must identify that resistance is happening. The tool of examen, used to note if there is resistance within personal self, leadership, or the soul of the congregation, is very helpful. It takes a discerning heart to notice if others are experiencing resistance. Resistance can look like anger, fear, apathy, or procrastination. When you notice resistance within or beyond self, stay calm. Do not let others rile you up into argumentation. And do not convenience yourself that there are justifiable reasons that you cannot enter the process of deepening and expanding experiences of spiritual formation.

Another way of dealing with resistance and staying calm, which invites compassion to be lived, is to be that non-anxious presence. When we view resistance as a natural process, there is no need to demonize or say belittling things about others. As one seeks to stay calm in the face

---

29 Buckwell, *Rediscovering the Contemplative Tradition*, 116.

of resistance, intention is given to an interior scan. This interior scan provides a quick assessment if there are any prejudgments, listening filters, or narrow perspectives that need to be amended to fully receive the other. Once a quick interior assessment is complete, attention is turned beyond self to the others. The wonder is how best to support, receive, and love the other through the resistance for God's transfiguring metamorphosis to proceed.

A few skills to support and lead others through resistance come directly from the tools of spiritual direction training. Supporting another does not necessarily mean giving in to the resistant demands. Buoying up others through this transfiguring process can happen in many ways. Holy listening is a powerful tool to move toward release of resistance. Allowing story of the resistant person to be held lightly and fully received gifts him or her with a sense that his or her ideas and feelings are important. Further, the tool of three-way listening is vital to speaking with those who are resistant. Asking within our deepest heart how God loves the other, listens, and desires him or her to move beyond resistance is an utmost priority. Remember that this is God's process, and we are the vessels of God gifted with the compassion of Jesus to share with others.

The primary objective in dealing with resistance is to aid the resister in self-discovery of God's encircling love. To do this we move beneath the known layer of thoughts and words that entrap us with certain perspectives. Leading the community of individuals to see beyond the surface, as discussed earlier, is paramount to releasing resistance. Tools of spiritual direction training provide a safe, sacred space to be heard, accepted, and loved. This provides the opportunity for opposing parties to hear self, God, and others amid disorientation, institutional upheaval, theological disharmony, feelings of vulnerability, and loss of control.

In order to lead communities through resistance, it is very helpful to name the resistance. To name resistance helps the other (the resistant one) articulate what is happening within, and is best done in a very neutral way without pushing an agenda. This is very different than telling the other what he or she feels or that he or she is resistant. Helping people name their own resistance is a very powerful tool for creating authentic community.

There are many ways to assist people in naming resistance. Creative arts with colored pencils, even thinking about which color one would like to name the resistance, is helpful. When I worked for a season at a mental health and recovery ministry, the head clinician asked to meet with me. This psychotherapist had one question: "What was I doing that moved clients faster toward recovery and greater health than his highly trained social work-ers and counselors?" I did not have a clue and told him so. He suggested I tell him a few things I was doing with the clients. I began with the creative arts prayer, praying in color. When I finished, he said, "Now, I see." He further explained that coloring has been scientifically proven to open space within the brain. It gives clarity and focus, and has an immense calming effect. He described in detail how this creative art of coloring alters the brain state and opens the individual to new possibility. I wondered, Could coloring open us to greater receptivity to God's gentle whispers? He responded affirmatively, if one was to believe in such things.

Another technique of creative arts is the discovery of self-empowerment tools with the use of a hidden picture.[30] As clients searched for the hidden pictures embedded within the larger picture, they initially worked quietly on their own. Soon some were complaining it was too hard. Others sought out companions in the class to work together to discover the hidden whole-ness of the picture. Ultimately, the entire group worked co-operatively to discover the hidden pictures. During the debrief of the experience, after naming all the tools that had been used to discover the hidden pictures, the correlation between these tools and the process of recovery was made that helped to move the clients forward in wholeness of life. This is a hoped-for outcome of spiritual direction also.

Using creative arts to overcome resistance is a tricky thing. Creative arts often bring out cries of "Not me, I am no artist"; "I cannot possibly do that"; or "That is for children, not adults." And yet Jesus invites us to become like children as we move toward greater wholeness and traverse the resistances of disorienting and chaotic times.[31] The use of creative arts prayer and tools of spiritual direction training open the way for community to consider new possibilities.

Regardless of what tools are used to assist in the naming of resistance, it is always necessary to be truthful. There are no fires to put out in the process of morphing transfiguration. Take it slow, pray together, listen deeply with the inner ear of your hearts, and trust that God will open the way.

---

30 I, like many, was first introduced to hidden pictures as a child through *Highlights* magazine.

31 "[Jesus] called a child, whom he put among them, and said, 'Truly I tell you, unless you change and become like children, you will never enter the kingdom of heaven. Whoever becomes humble like this child is the greatest in the kingdom of heaven'" (Matt 18:2–4).

Once resistance is named, it can be dealt with in a healthy manner. Keeping things hidden only opens the way for resistance to fester and infect others through the years of ministry. Remember the illustration of the congregation that had the celebrity to speak against an unpopular war? Years later, the incident was still lingering in the hearts of some people. Together, in community of two or more, we can discern how best to move forward through this resistance. Working through resistance in the metamorphic process as all voices are heard provides opportunity for the community to move toward greater Christlikeness.

One final thought about dealing with resistance: Please do not take resistance personally. On occasion, the resisters may hope you take it personally, unable to move forward. But in the grand scheme of God's design it really is not about you. The resister has some interior work to do. You may be able to assist with that; you may not. Is the other's mental or emotional state such that they need a referral to another kind of practitioner? When a person or community begins to feel heard in their own struggle, there is potential to move toward God's new preferred future.

Effects on the Congregational Vision of Ministry

As the stories unfold, the potential of spiritually forming tools of spiritual direction training is clearly seen. These tools impact how one relates to others in ministry. Enhancement of communication, listening, and discernment skills are foundational gifts of this training. Small groups become an opportunity for group spiritual direction. Learning how to ask clear-conscience formational questions, waiting, and being comfortable with silence all aid in deepening a heartfelt presence of God's burning passion within community. Every facet of training in spiritual direction increases one's ability to listen beyond the surface to the interior heart. Training in three-way listening affects all arenas of ministry.

Vision is potentially birthed from the Word of God through the shared practice of listening deeply to the biblical Word and allowing it to transfigure community. Empowerment from God is awakened as the church incrementally moves from disorientation and chaos through this process of heightened search to a new change of consciousness.

All these tools from spiritual direction training open the way for the congregation to become a safe and sacred place for others. Slowly, over time, resistances can be embraced and released as God leads the congregation into God's most translucent place of metamorphosis. The next sections of this book provide testimony to the transfiguring power of the tools of spiritual direction. We notice that all people have the potential to be transfigured through the implementation of tools from spiritual direction training as we look at the two sides of leadership. But before we move to the heartbeat of personal leadership, let us pause for contemplative reflection on section 3 with examen.

Spiritual Direction Readiness Assessment and Congregational Examen

At the end of each section of this book is a Spiritual Direction Readiness Assessment and Congregational Examen. As mentioned earlier, consider creating a portfolio, either on the computer or with pencil and paper. Within this portfolio, record your responses to the assessment and examen. At the end of this book, review your portfolio of responses. Ponder how God is inviting you further into the metamorphosis process for leadership and within the church.

Section 3's discernment and examen focus is about the soul of the congregation with consideration of leadership within the congregation. Consider if there are resistances limiting the leaps of inward and outward expression of Divine compassion and spiritual growth.

WORKSHEET OF EXAMEN: TRAINING THE HEART

Congregational Leadership Assessment

A. Know Thyself
    a. Have you ever been or are you stuck? What was that like for you?
    b. What do you do when you become unstuck?

    c.   What specifically do you do to open the way for the congregation to claim their belovedness?

    d.   How comfortable are you with silence? If distractions intrude on your silence, how do you regain attentive listening?

    e.   Have you ever experienced the "whiteout blizzard" of the soul?

B.   Non-Anxious Presence

    a.   Do you tend to bypass or walk through the difficulties of life?

    b.   What causes you to become anxious?

    c.   How do you practice detachment from anxiety?

C.   Holy Listening and Storytelling

    a.   How comfortable are you with each level of storytelling and listening?

    b.   How does your counter-story affect your listening experience?

    c.   Are there topics of conversation to which you are not able to listen?

    d.   What listening filters shade your worldview?

D.   Resistance

    a.   When have you experienced being resistant?

    b.   How do you overcome your personal resistance?

Please close your time of prayer with this or one of your own prayers.

> Holy God, One in Three and Three in One, we love you. I love you. You know the struggles of my heart as I yearn for expanded awareness of you. I did not even know that I was yearning so deeply. Accept my yearnings and open my heart so that I may live as you love among your people. Grant our congregation and me freedom to release what holds it captive and move into your greatest desires. Together may we become new in your energy as we live, love, and dance with the flaming love of God transfiguring our lives. Amen.

Congregational Examen

A.   Know Thyself

    a.   Has the congregation ever experienced a time of stuckness?

    b.   If so, what was that like?

    c.   How has the congregation overcome stuckness?

    d.   When you examine the congregation, how do the parishioners live their truest identity as God's beloved?

    e.   How comfortable is the congregation with silence?

    f.   What do you do to aid the congregation with silence and release of distractions?

    g.   Has the congregation ever experienced the "whiteout blizzard" of the soul? What happened, and how did they move through it?

B. Non-Anxious Presence

    a.   When does the congregation become non-anxious?

    b.   What is that like?

C. Holy Listening and Storytelling

    a.   How comfortable is the congregation with each level of storytelling and listening?

    b.   How does the congregational counter-story influence listening skills?

    c.   What are the congregational listening filters?

D. Resistance

    a.   When does resistance arise within the congregation?

    b.   What do you as leader do to assist the congregation going through resistance?

    c.   How does the congregation collectively practice the tools of spiritual direction, daily prayer, and examen?

Interface of Personal and Congregational Responses

A. Are the leader and congregation in the same position of transfiguring metamorphosis?

B. What similarities do you notice between the leader and congregation?

C. What is different between the leader and congregation?

D. What stage of awakening do you discern for yourself and for the congregation?

    a.   *Disorientation:* How do you and the congregation experience chaos and confusion?

    b.   *Heightened Search for God:* How have you and the congregation noticed an increased intentionality and search for the voice of truth—God's Divine presence in the midst of leadership, everyday life, and within the inner understanding of faith?

    c.   *Change of Consciousness:* What new ways of prayer have taken hold within the congregation? Is the congregation ready to live new things? How is leadership and the congregation expanding new wings for flight?

E. What is an invitation from God for moving *into* a transfiguring metamorphosis?
F. What is the invitation from God for *descending* toward the heart of God into greater metamorphosis and awakening?

Please close your time of prayer with this or one of your own prayers.

Holy God, One in Three and Three in One; we love you. You know the struggles of our hearts as we yearn for expanded awareness of you. We did not even know that we were yearning so deeply. Accept our yearnings and open our hearts so that we may live as you love among your people. Grant our congregation freedom to release what holds it captive and move into your greatest desires. Together may we become new in your eyes as we live, love, and dance with the flaming love of God transfiguring our lives. Amen.

Four

LIVING PASSION OF THE AWAKENED HEART

Butterfly Stage I: Awakened in God's Time

After the work of metamorphosis within the chrysalis, the butterfly hangs upside down until the opportune time of emergence from the chrysalis. The monarch's chrysalis by this time is transparent, so all can view the beautiful new life. But the butterfly is not yet set free for flight. There are restraints that still bind the wings from flight.

This transfiguring process of metamorphosis is just that, a process. It takes time. As leaders become an impassioned, translucent force of love for the congregations, congregations have the potential to open the way for new possibilities in God. This morphing process of a congregation is literally viewed by all who gaze upon the church. There is no containing the energy, illuminating love, and light of Christ as a congregation becomes effervescent in God. No longer does the congregation strive so hard to help people know that they are loved through programmatic focus. As this transfiguring process infuses the soul of the congregation, the winsome spirit of translucent God-love radiates from parishioners.

Inspiration comes to us through stories of a transformed life. Participants from spiritual direction training programs and classes from the Louisiana area training program, CenterQuest, and seminaries tell their yearnings, hopes, and dreams with a wide-angle perspective of Divine grace. We will hear stories that address these questions: As one personally experiences the teachable skills of contemplative listening, what shifts within to open heart hospitality? How does spiritual direction training transgress the division between conservative evangelical, traditional, and progressive? How does inward formation affect external action and mission of the church?

Through spiritual direction training, Sally (not her real name) discovered how to abide daily in God. There is a fullness of God's activity that she had not previously noticed before.

> This becomes a source for all my coping skills. I remember a professor of mine who had a major crisis with one of his children during class and he was called to the emergency. One of his students said to him afterwards, "Dr. Edwards [name changed], you must have been really praying hard all the way to the hospital." The professor looked over at him and said, "No, to tell you the truth I wasn't. I know my Father and my Father knows me and he knew exactly what I needed, and I didn't have to tell God anything." This is how my hunger is nourished now through my daily reflection time. When difficult things arise, I am prepared in God. It is not a last-minute rush to call upon God and ask for prayers for an outcome I desire. These daily reflection times, the opportunity to open space for God, have become my routine daily diet. . . .
>
> You cannot make connection if you are moving at too fast a pace. . . . All of the training is a process, and the process doesn't end just because the class sessions end. God is still forming me.[1]

"Not a last-minute rush to call upon God"—what powerful words. That means no longer needing to have quick drive-thru kinds of prayers at the last minute, pleading with God for the outcome we deem best. As the pace of life slows, we are nourished by God. The converse is true also. As we are nourished by God, the pace of life slows. This is the first of many stories that highlight the power of a transfigured life through the metamorphic process of spiritual direction training.

---

1   Buckwell, *Rediscovering the Contemplative Tradition*, 94.

Stories of a Transfigured Life

The hunger deepens and is nourished as participants complete the training in spiritual direction. Each life becomes grounded with a new and renewed foundational perspective of prayer, life, and community. Each person passionately desired to tell his or her story and how he or she moved through disorientation and chaos to resurrection possibility. Each story is not just an individual story but part of God's greatest story. All names have been changed.

Sally

Testimonies to the power of spiritual direction training are very heartfelt, so humbling, and authentic. It is necessary to be able to articulate the shift in how one relates to others with the tools of spiritual direction training. Once articulated, the shift becomes the foundation for living. This deters one from too easily slipping back into his or her old familiar ways.

> I have learned how to help draw out the story from the other. I encourage them by saying, "This is what I am hearing from you; pay attention to that." I am much quicker now to tell people to trust their heart. My [leadership] effectiveness has increased greatly as I feel less responsible for the people and let God lead their lives. I am just holding that mirror up the best I can so they can notice God in their lives for themselves.
>
> The people I work with, and [I], now really trust God's wisdom. I have gained a confidence I think I worked hard to compensate for before.[2]

Sally names an emerging distinction for those trained in spiritual direction. Deep trust in God lessens attachments to one's own will and personal emotions, and creates a non-anxious presence for conversation with others. The non-anxious listening provides a place of encouragement for others' authentic faith formation and deepened self-awareness. This deep trust in God gives rise to confidence.

> I understand the whole sense of being God's instrument better. I love the image of spiritual direction with three chairs in the room: me, the other person, and God. . . . My vocational call has gained so

---

2   Buckwell, *Rediscovering the Contemplative Tradition*, 95.

much clarity. Spiritual direction is now a part of everything I do in ministry. . . . I live and work more in the present moment. This is a huge shift for me. I have probably spent most of my adult life trying to get to the next station in life and wanting to be somewhere else. Now I trust God's voice, even knowing there are other voices that clamor for my attention. Even in this last year, when I pushed myself almost to a breaking point—and it wasn't the first time. . . . All of this has brought me to a point of really living what I have learned. And what I have learned is how important pace and self-care is. I knew it before, but I couldn't live it.[3]

There is a subtle shift that Sally expresses in the above statements. She talks about the use of language: before training she had the words, and now she lives the essence of the words.

Often before, I, like others, just thought of going on retreat to get renewed, fill up the spiritual gas tank again. . . . But that doesn't change the way that we live. I needed to be changed, formed into a new way of living and ministry. There is now no way to go back to the hectic pace.[4]

Spiritual direction is all about being open to God and allowing God to lead. It brings us into a humble place of "standing in the holy."

This training leads me and my colleagues to be more authentic. To be completely honest, in my opinion, the way we pamper and honor people in certain roles sends the wrong message. Grace and humility are important, but they are not our doing. They are God's forming within us. Often, we try to work at being gracious and humble as byproducts of devotion. But these two gifts as I have experienced come from standing in the presence of the holy.[5]

Juliet

Teresa of Avila and John of the Cross have transformed my life. I was a great wine connoisseur and had become very dependent on it for coping with the hectic schedule of ministry and life. During my

---

3   Buckwell, *Rediscovering the Contemplative Tradition*, 96.
4   Buckwell, 96.
5   Buckwell, 97.

spiritual direction training I came face to face with this reality. It was when we studied "The Dark Night of the Soul" and Teresa of Avila's Interior Castle[6] that I began to realize the strength was coming from within for me to be able to overcome any kind of compulsive behavior and addictive behavior or any kind of thing that was pulling me away from God or fuzzing my picture of reality.

The progression of Juliet's spiritual journey has enabled her to make herself even more available and authentic to others in their spiritual journeys. This is a vital step in learning to translate what is learned personally in spiritual direction training to the local ministry setting. From her interior journey, Juliet's exterior life shifted, and leadership effectiveness has increased.

The term *companioning* has been really life changing for me. It has shifted the way I look at being with other people . . . I gained the freedom and trust of God, realizing I didn't always have to have the answers and didn't always have to have a perfect word to say. By nature, I am a fixer. Half of my life has been spent trying to fix people's pains, hurts, and problems. . . . Rather than trying to tell them what I see happening in their life or what I feel God is doing in their life, I listen to what they feel and what they see. I am more encouraging of them to seek their own answers. . . . This companionship became, through my training, a new call of ministry for my life.

Juliet has realized her own habitual way of reacting to situations and people around her. She was a "fixer." Culturally, we reward people for fixing our problems. Generally, people prefer to ask for advice in finding solutions to problems, which encourages the fixer role within community. Unfortunately, when things do not go as we hoped, this can lead to blame. We often find it much easier to blame the fixer for giving us the wrong advice. Spiritual direction has the potential to curb one's propensity to fix others so that one is no longer tempted to offer the perceived best solutions.[7] The gifts of our availability and openness as believers provide great opportunity for each person to become a companion on the journey with others.

---

6   From the 1500s, Teresa of Ávila's Interior Castle is a model for looking at and naming the process of spiritual formation in one's life. For further information, see Teresa of Ávila, translated by Mirabai Starr. 2003. *The Interior Castle*. New York: Riverhead Books.

7   Buckwell, *Rediscovering the Contemplative Tradition*, 99.

Together, we notice and name how God companions us through life and in community.

> Spiritual direction [tools] have helped me to be more accepting and tolerant in seeing all equal before God. I used to be more critical and quicker to judge. It is very humbling when you look back and see where God has brought you. And God does this for everyone.[8]

CenterQuest Participants

Information only has polarized the conversations of theology and faith. Yet, there is great potential for closing the gap and even crossing the theological divide with spiritual direction training. As part of the teaching team for CenterQuest, we interface with people from around the world. These participants have diverse theological understandings, and yet the same God is forming the participants' inward being. A participant writes after just one month of training how transforming it has become for him. This participant comes from rural Nebraska.

> My starting point in the process of learning to see was I realized I needed to unlearn some things I thought I already knew. I needed to confess I was blind.
> I thought by reading the materials and watching the videos I would . . . learn how to do something new. . . . I thought in dualistic categories. I fragmented spiritual growth into a to-do list to become a victorious Christian (whatever that means). I thought if I consumed the right information and did it, I would reach a higher level of spiritual enlightenment.
> Little did I know the pathway to a new consciousness was a descent into a beginner's mind. First, I had to become like a child. I needed to see as a child—think like a child. To awaken out of my sleepwalking, as Rohr describes, I need to learn how to see.[9]
> Experiencing the silent land through contemplative prayer has revealed an awareness of the Presence. . . . During the moments of stillness, the separation of self from thoughts and feelings has

---

8   Buckwell, *Rediscovering the Contemplative Tradition*, 100.
9   Richard Rohr. 1999. *Everything Belongs: The Gift of Contemplative Prayer.* Chestnut Ridge, NY: Crossroad Publishing.

been transformational. I've awakened spiritually to see my ego-self in a whole new light. During ordinary life, I'm observing how the false self is exerting itself in relationships and my reactions to circumstances.

I have begun to see that one source of my blindness is my identification with the intellectual illusions of who I think I am. . . . I've built my first half-life around the self-image of "I am success-ful," or "My performance makes me lovable," or "I've got my life together."

These images blur my ability to see myself as a beloved child of God. After years and years of looking at life through these illusions, it feels as though cataracts are removed from my eyes. It's been a humiliating and frightening experience to see how much of my life I lived trying to act out these illusions. I feel as though I'm on the edge of seeing myself hidden in Christ for the very first time.

Another CenterQuest participant writes of her experience after just two months of training. She is from Bandung, West Java, Indonesia.

Walking through the [Contemplative Prayer 2 class] is nothing more than to train my spiritual ear to listen deeper, broader, and better to God, to myself, to others, and to nature. Practicing different ways of listening through *Lectio* series was a transformative experience for me. . . . Added *Audio Divina* to *Visio Divina*, to do *Lectio* . . . , all of these practice help me to integrate my spiritual seeing and hear-ing. . . . Before I take this course, I have been well trained to read and digest the Bible with an analytical thinking, . . . to pray with the words. . . . While I reflect on my prayer life [these] images come to my mind: at the past I come to God with my shopping list; and God was like a vending machine, where we can get what we want by [inserting] a prayer. I never learn how to listen [to] God in a prayer or in a silence, I never pray with my [senses], don't know how to do walking prayer, how to do Christian meditation and to pray with the art, with my hands and feet, and so on. I have to admit these spiri-tual practices [changed] me tremendously. It turned the way how I read my Bible, to pray and to do my daily spiritual walks and to deal with life, myself, ministry, others, and nature in a 180-degree [way]. I could say, what I have learned in these several months [is greater] than what I have learned in my whole life.

From Alberta, Canada, we continue our discovery from tools of spiritual direction training as this participant tells how intentional, consistent practice of spiritual disciplines form a foundation for spiritual direction.

> I began this course with some confidence that my previously engrained praxis of centering prayer and private *Lectio Divina* were serving me well and that I had a good handle on listening to God and the word. . . . I am even more of a beginner than I thought I was. . . . The eighteen-inch journey of my faith from my head to my heart is far longer than I expected it would be. . . .
>
> It is a relief to relax into the truth [that] God's always present rather than to fret over whether my mind is silent enough, whether I am sensing Holy Presence or making up "spiritual feelings" with my imagination, or any of my other head-based wrestling matches.

These testimonies of transformed lives encourage the possibility of spiritual direction as foundation for the transfiguring process of metamorphosis. New power of God illumines the lives of those who internalize the tools of spiritual direction training.

The Power of a Transformed Life

Many laypeople, like Annie (not her real name), have deep, rich, surprising, and "strange" experiences of God. Who does the layperson turn to for conversation to deepen and broaden his or her understanding of God? . . .

> The person who came to mind was my pastor. We had spoken a couple of times before. When I went to see him, he listened attentively and then began his counseling mode. I wasn't broken, I didn't need [to be] fixed. I only wanted someone to help me understand this deep spiritual experience I had. . . .

Annie's experience of God was so profound in her life that it led her in a totally new direction for life. Her lament from her earliest experience of not being received by her pastor when she needed help in discerning what God was speaking to her still shapes how she dedicates her life. . . .

> People still ask me what I do. I tell them I am the director of spiritual formation. But it is a whole new vocabulary for the congregation. Most people are skeptical of it because it is not known. They see

it as touchy feely—men especially see it as touchy feely; it is very threatening.

Annie states that spiritual direction is a "whole new vocabulary" for the church people and the clergy with whom she works. I wonder how the church has drifted so far from heart-knowing. Has the vocabulary been co-opted? Has the intense challenge of words such as *discipline, prayer, silence,* and *intimacy with God* been reduced so that God language is more controllable? Have believers become so uncomfortable with the mystery of God that we have shied away from the hiddenness of God?

> The way my ministry developed is that I started out part time, focused on spiritual direction. I began doing one-on-one direction and having monthly group times of reflection using *Lectio Divina* readings with Lent and Advent text. I was getting a good turnout. Then I realized that within the church structure what I was doing [was perceived] more like, "Okay, we got a little spiritual direction thing on the side going on over there." One of the associate pastors said this ministry "was sort of like a boutique ministry." What does that mean? Spiritual direction is a place to get your hair done?[10]

The success of a program of spiritual direction as opposed to creating a foundational stance can stymie rather than illumine the congregation. It makes a drastic difference in how the ministry of spiritual direction is viewed if it is an aside program of the church rather than foundational to the congregation. This influences how much the community is willing to tolerate and consent to the mysteriousness of God's interior movement in the lives of the people and the community.

> Three years later, . . . I am in a really difficult position, as a lay-staff person, with clergy not understanding my ministry of spiritual direction and spiritual formation. . . . It is not a program where you take a spiritual gifts test and know what you are supposed to go do. Formation is all about support, listening, and discernment. It is a lifestyle, not program and numbers. It is a reshaping of the interior life to live and breathe and grow and transform a congregation.[11]

---

10 Buckwell, *Rediscovering the Contemplative Tradition,* 106–7.
11 Buckwell, 109.

The intent of spiritual direction is to deepen awareness of God within the storyteller. A word of wisdom from those that train spiritual directors: just because one trains with the tools of spiritual direction does not mean one is called to be a spiritual director. However, everyone may benefit from spiritual direction training, which can enable congregations to greater intention in formally and informally training the hearts of congregants. This leads us to even greater acceptance of God's mystery. A discernment question for the church is, Has the church sought to domesticate God and avoid mystery?

Spiritual direction within the Protestant tradition is a new thing. Resistance is one way of dealing with new things. Story after story tells the agonizing feelings of those who seek to faithfully live their call of spiritual direction within the church structure. Several who have been interviewed have used words like *persecution, alienation,* and *isolation.* Yet they also experience such strength from God that there is no other way they would shape their ministry.

Through the ages of history, those who sought to reform the church have been persecuted. Wisdom from the *ammas* and *abbas,* Benedict, Ignatius, Teresa of Ávila, John of the Cross, and John and Charles Wesley, show us the reality of prophetic voices seeking to call the church back to stability through the transfiguring process of metamorphosis. How will the church again become the voice calling new life forth from disorientation, inviting people into heightened awareness of God's presence among humanity? Annie continues her story.

> Honestly, if God had not taken me through that dark night and been so intimate and even done more miracles with me . . . , I would have never made it. . . . Because without God's wisdom and courage carrying me, I could not do this. I could not do this physically, mentally, or emotionally if it were not God's.[12]

Companions for the journey are vital. It is necessary for everyone to have a safe community to talk through the hurts, pains, and attacks that may be endured when faithfully living the call to re-formation in a disoriented culture. Is there a way for the church to become a culture of safety?

> Many of the ones who have experienced the spiritual direction training take . . . anger and run it through a refining process before it gets out in the stated feelings to the public. It is like pushing your emotions through a sieve of some kind and makes that product on

---

12 Buckwell, 111.

the other side much finer—the anger then is not just an explosion of all the rocks and bullets projecting out on others.... People were more deeply conformed to the image of Christ, ... It is becoming a gentler soul in the moment of crisis. It is not any less intense a soul—but gentler in its presentation.[13]

"One gains a gentler presentation of self to the world, for the world." In a world where there is much confusion, chaos, random violence, and terrorism, this is extremely important. The more we can love as Jesus' loves, the greater the translucent love of Christ shines.

There is a significant difference between formational and informational ways of dealing with concepts, topics, and issues. These are two distinctive ways of learning from and communicating with one another. We can talk and debate all we want around ministry issues. We can proof-text each point in our argument with the Bible, which pits one theological position against another. This is informational learning and conversation. This linear kind of thought takes the form of accepting that there is a correct and given solution to the topic at hand.

Each one of us is a person with varying degrees of personal leadership qualities. As section 5 shows, professional leadership can only move as far as our personal leadership allows. Use of the Diamond Leadership Assessment opens discovery for how the tools of spiritual direction training enhance our personal leadership. But before moving to section 5, please pause and reflect on the Spiritual Direction Readiness Assessment and Congregational Examen from the stories of a transfigured life.

Spiritual Direction Readiness Assessment and Congregational Examen

At the end of each section of this book Is a Spiritual Direction Readiness Assessment and Congregational Examen. As mentioned earlier, consider creating a portfolio, either on the computer or with pencil and paper. Within this portfolio, record your responses to the assessment and examen. At the end of this book, review your portfolio of responses. Ponder how God is inviting you further into the metamorphosis process for leadership and within the church.

---

13 Buckwell, 119.

For section 4 the readiness assessment and examen section provides questions pondering the gift of God's presence amid the current reality of leader and congregation. Are we ready to make an interior shift in the soul of the congregation? The implementation of individual, group, and corporate spiritual direction will be considered.

WORKSHEET OF EXAMEN: HOW IS GOD WHISPERING TO YOUR HEART?

Personal Leadership Assessment

A. On the spectrum of faith, where are you?
    a. Encased in the security of the chrysalis
    b. Praying transfiguring prayers daily so that God's beauty shines forth
    c. Finding courage to break out of old ways
    d. Actively stepping into God's new life potential
B. Praying with past participants: Review the section "Stories of a Transfigured Life."
    a. Choose one testimony of how spiritual direction has affected a past participant's life.
    b. Upon the first reading of this testimony, what word or phrase catches your heart?
    c. Read the same testimony a second time. How does the testimony intersect with your experience of life in this moment or your desire for living prayer into the future?
    d. Read the same testimony a third time. What is the invitation of God to you from this participant's witness? Could it be an invitation to be or to do something?[14]

---

14 I first learned of these questions for modified Examen from the *Companion in Christ* series published by Upper Room Books.

Please close your time of prayer with this or one of your own prayers.

> Creator God, Redeeming Word of Life, awaken my sleeping spirit that I may dance with you into new steps of love and life. Move me from where I have been to the overflowing gifts of your power and presence anointing my inward being. Lead me as I gently move into this new crucible for my life. Truly, I seek to leave the chaos and disorientation behind and open my heart to the power of your illuminating spirit. Ignite my imagination and courage for action. May flames of your passion be awakened within my heart so that others may be drawn to your Holy presence. Amen.

Congregational Examen

A. On the spectrum of faith, where is the congregation?
   a. Encased in the security of the chrysalis
   b. Praying transfiguring prayers daily so that God's beauty shines forth
   c. Finding courage to break out of old ways
   d. Actively stepping into God's new life potential
B. Praying with past participants: Review the section "Stories of a Transfigured Life."
   a. Choose one past participant's testimony that resonates with the experience of the congregation.
   b. Upon the first reading of this testimony, what word or phrase catches the congregation's heart?
   c. Read the same testimony a second time. How does his or her testimony intersect with the congregational experience or desire for deepened prayer?
   d. Read the same testimony a third time. What is the invitation of God to the congregation? Could it be an invitation to be or to do something?

Interface of Personal and Congregational Responses

A. Are the leader and congregation in the same position of transfiguring metamorphosis?
B. What similarities between the leader and congregation do you notice?
C. What is different between the leader and congregation?
D. What stage of awakening do you discern for yourself and for the congregation?

a. *Disorientation:* How do you and the congregation experience chaos and confusion?
b. *Heightened Search for God:* How have you and the congregation noticed an increased intentionality and search for the voice of truth, God's Divine presence in the midst of leadership, everyday life, and within the inner understanding of faith?
c. *Change of Consciousness:* What new ways of prayer have taken hold within the congregation? Is the congregation ready to live new things? How is leadership and the congregation expanding new wings for flight?

E. What is an invitation from God for moving forward *into* a transfiguring metamorphosis?
F. What is the invitation from God for *descending* toward the heart of God into greater metamorphosis and awakening?

Please close your time of prayer with this or one of your own prayers.

Creator God, Redeeming Word of Life, awaken our sleeping spirit that we may dance with you into new steps of love and life. Move us from where we have been to the overflowing gifts of your power and presence anointing our inward being. Lead us gently so we may move into this new crucible for the soul of the congregation. Truly, we seek to leave the chaos and disorientation behind and open our hearts to the power of your illuminating spirit. Ignite our imagination and courage for action. May flames of your passion be awakened within the soul of the congregation so that others may be drawn to your Holy presence. Amen.

Five

REALITY, POSSIBILITY, OR PIPE DREAM?

Butterfly Stage II: Transformed and Ready

After the metamorphosis, the butterfly waits inside the transparent chrysalis. I wonder if the butterfly assesses its new tools. Will anyone recognize the soul of the butterfly as that which was in the caterpillar? The butterfly must grow into its new understanding of self and trust its new way of moving through life. Personal leadership is imperative for the completion of metamorphic transfiguration.

We have spoken of the congregational reorientation through group and corporate spiritual direction, yet in a very real sense the congregation is made up of individuals. Spiritual direction is always an individual pursuit. Each one of us expands awareness and deepens experiences of God personally. As more and more individuals have this experience within a community, the congregation is poised for descending further toward the heart of God through formation. As individuals within a church venture forth into heightened search for God, it is the personal leadership skills that move the congregation in formation. We may echo the imagined butterfly's worries. Will we be recognized with our new way of illuminating Christlikeness to the world? How will we gain a strength of inward personhood as we move forward in formation?

Section 5 looks at personal leadership for both staff and parishioners. Personal leadership, integrity, ethics, and power are always the foundation of professional leadership. We will explore the "inner side of greatness" with Peter Koestenbaum's Diamond Leadership Assessment. It is through increased personal leadership that the wonder is raised if transfiguring the soul of the congregation could be a reality, possibility, or just a pipe dream.

The cry of the church is heard as we live on the edge of God's new way of learning and being community. This cry is echoed with seminary students when assigned a formational project. At first, they grumble that the assignment of a Rule of Life Assessment seems too simplistic. By the mid-semester check-in, those who have consistently adhered to the rhythm of extended time for prayer discover the truth—the truth that it takes great intentionality and desire to focus on prayer in the midst of a busy life. They also discover the truth that God becomes present in new, unimagined ways as tools from spiritual direction training are plumbed. At the end of the semester, 95 to 98 percent of students articulate how transforming the class project has been for them. This transfiguration has occurred personally and within ministry leadership. One student testifies to the lasting impact of the class even after graduating seminary and serving in ministry full time for several years.

> I would like . . . to tell you how much your courses meant to me and how they have truly marked my life. . . . The blessing of sitting in silence before the Lord. The joy of seeking to live in spiritual simplicity. The essential position of maintaining a peaceful center focused on Jesus—these are just a few of the things I have embraced from your classes. Interestingly, these and some of the other spiritual disciplines have not only helped me in my walk in general but also have given me a heightened awareness of when I am in an environment of unrest, frenetic activity, focus on "many things" instead of on the essential (the one thing that is needed, Lk 10:42). This is good—it protects me from myself since if I am not careful, I can easily become caught up in the rat race of needing to be constantly "doing" something and the "tyranny of the urgent" which seems to plague so many ministries! (These are the words of someone who has suffered "burn-out" twice in the past!)[1]

1   JoAnn Gladd, Ashland Seminary student email. October 18, 2019. Used with permission.

Are the rigors of academia lost with this focus on formation? No. The students' numerous papers, research, and writings are just as prolific as in their other classes.

Possibility

Possibility abounds for creating a safe place for authentic soul-sharing through the metamorphosis process. Why do we need a safe space? I am reminded of the metaphor for the soul that Palmer describes, which highlights why sacred, safe space is so necessary.

> Like a wild animal, the soul is tough, resilient, resourceful, savvy, and self-sufficient: it knows how to survive in hard places . . . something that knew how to stay alive. . . . That something [is the] tough and tenacious soul.
>
> Yet despite its toughness, the soul is also shy. Just like a wild animal, it seeks safety in the dense underbrush, especially when other people are around. If we want to see a wild animal, we know that the last thing we should do is go crashing through the woods yelling for it to come out. But if we will walk quietly into the woods, sit patiently at the base of a tree, breathe with the earth, and fade into our surroundings, the wild creature we seek might put in an appearance.[2]

Threats to the cocooning caterpillar abound. The "chalcid wasp . . . parasitizes the monarch when it's in chrysalis form. Before the chrysalis has a chance to harden, the chalcid wasp pierces the surface and lays eggs, sometimes hundreds of them. The chalcid larvae kill the developing pupa and eventually exit the chrysalis as adult wasps."

Baumle, *The Monarch*, 88.

The shy, tenacious soul of our being yearns for safe, sacred space. Spiritual direction and holy listening create inward sacred space with integrity, ethics,

---

2   Parker Palmer. 2004. *A Hidden Wholeness: The Journey Toward an Undivided Life: Welcoming and Weaving Community in a Wounded World.* San Francisco: Jossey-Bass. Page 58.

and personal power. The shy, wild soul can come out and pray together without fear of judgment, jokes, and injustices. As the world reorients through the pandemic and civil protests, it is a prime time for creating this personal interior space for receiving others. It is not just personal physical distance, but our spirit breathes deeply of God when ample room is left for God to swell among us.

Heart Leadership

Personal authenticity is at the heartbeat of good leadership. Peter Koestenbaum, business executive and author of *Leadership: The Inner Side of Greatness*, assesses leadership as illustrated in figure 7.[3]

Figure 7. The Diamond Leadership Model

ETHICS
Be of Service

REALITY
Have No Illusions

GREATNESS
*Potential for
Extraordinary Results*

VISION
Thinking Big & New

COURAGE
*Act with Sustained
Initiative*

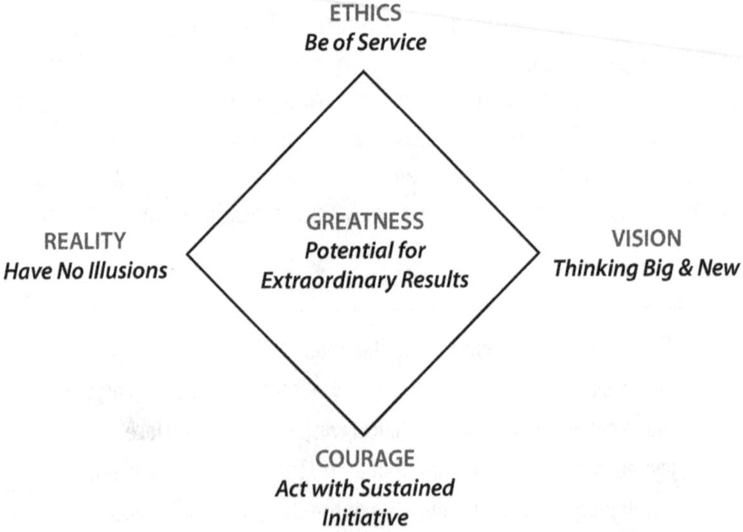

The Leadership Diamond® is a registered trademark, and Philosophy-in-Business™ and PiB™ are trademarks of Peter Koestenbaum. Copyright © 2002.[4]

---

3   Peter Koestenbaum. 2002. *Leadership: The Inner Side of Greatness, A Philosophy for Leaders.* San Francisco: Jossey-Bass.

4   This illustration was downloaded from the Internet resource at http://www.pib .net/model.htm (accessed July 12, 2007). *PiB.NET,* "Diamond Leadership Model," http://www.pib.net/model.htm.

Each point of the Diamond Leadership Model is an attribute for interior and exterior formation. If one of the points is underdeveloped and not strengthened to full potential, then the individual has room in that specific area for personal growth and formation. Leadership abilities are diminished with an imbalance of skill. Figure 8 provides a picture of imbalanced personal and professional leadership.[5]

Figure 8. Imbalanced Leadership Skills

Examples of imbalance in the required characteristics:

What does your personal diamond look like? You may access the PIP assessment at www.pib.net/assessment.php. Once you discern your leadership diamond, you have the opportunity to strengthen personal and professional relationships. When this diamond of leadership qualities is overlaid with the tools of spiritual direction training, one gains a heart transformed in personal leadership.

Transfigured individuals transform culture, thus creating a different ethos within the greater community. Koestenbaum states: "Culture consists of unspoken expectations and invisible contracts, but it packs enormous emotional power, both positive and negative. . . . Strategy is mechanical and if necessary, can be bought. Culture, by contrast, is personal and is brought into being only through unusual personalities—ultimately, only through character. Like love, it is beyond purchase."[6]

The transfiguring tools of spiritual direction training and participation in spiritual direction have the potential to transform culture. To develop personal heart leadership, one must deepen all four aspects of leadership strategy in the Diamond Leadership Model through three-way listening. This

---

5   Buckwell, *Rediscovering the Contemplative Tradition*, 142.
6   Koestenbaum, *Leadership*, 57.

places God authentically at the heart of an individual life and of community life. Craig Emerick, once visiting faculty at Garrett-Evangelical Theological Seminary, called this inner side of the leadership diamond "soulfulness."

If one consents to do this interior work on the basis of a soul-deep knowing, integrity, and deep regard for others through ethics, new and renewed priorities of life arise. It is here the metamorphosis of transfiguration radiates from each life. As these individuals congregate, the church culture may molt into the greatest transparency of God's brilliant love light. With this foundation for forming community and individuals, new ways of creating a safe space for others to express their deepest desires develop.

Integrity and Ethics

The issue of dualistic relationship quickly arises when one begins identifying clergy as spiritual directors. The dualism of relationship occurs because the congregational pastor is first called to pastor the congregation—the whole congregation. In that role, the pastor is teacher, preacher, counselor, spiritual companion, friend, manager, administrator, and worship director. The pastor is to shepherd the people into deepened relationship with God. Tilden Edwards says, "Clergy in congregations are very busy and don't have time to see people on an individual basis, except for a one-shot affair. They can bring a deeper spiritual dimension to those one-shot affairs, but that is not classical ongoing spiritual direction."[7]

If a clergyperson is seeing someone from the congregation in spiritual direction, there may come a time when that individual needs skills other than three-way listening from the pastor. In those moments, the pastor must switch from the mode of deep listener to another role of teacher, comforter, and pray-er, or whatever the pastoral need is in that moment. Tilden Edwards cautions about the ethical implication of this one-on-one model in congregations. "It . . . could conceivably lead to a certain psychological jealousy within the congregation." Edwards imagines what a parishioner could claim of the clergy doing ongoing spiritual direction with just a few people in the congregation: that the clergyperson "has time for those two or three people but he [or she] doesn't have time for me." This is the same ethical issue raised by Rupert, a staff person from the Louisiana program: "It quickly became for me an ethical issue. How could I spend my time focusing on

---

7   Buckwell, *Rediscovering the Contemplative Tradition*, 148.

individual one-on-one spiritual direction when there was an entire congregation thirsting for a more intimate relationship with God?"[8]

Although there are these realistic and ethical cautions, Spirit-formed and Spirit-led persons trained as spiritual directors can strengthen local congregational ministry. According to Parker Palmer, this training increases the sense of authenticity within the spiritual life and relationship with God. As the inward nature is formed more nearly in the image of Christ, outwardly expressed roles, attitudes, and deeds are clarified. Additionally, the leader "could be more help to these soul and role issues that I think are vexing for a lot of people."[9] Widely teaching and experiencing the tools from spiritual direction training within a congregation potentially morphs community-clarifying soul and role issues. This intentional distribution of power and authority empowers the community in authentic spiritual formation and companionship.

Timing is everything. "In the fall, the wheels of migration have already been set in motion before the adult monarch emerges from its chrysalis. Even while it was still in its latter stages as a caterpillar, it was already being determined whether or not it would be emerging as a migrating butterfly."

Baumle, *The Monarch*, 37.

Power

The issue of power is vital to the wholeness and health of individuals and community. Many people feel powerless, which, as we have seen, can lead to resistance. The goal is with increase of personal power that people live

---

8   Buckwell, 148.
9   Buckwell, 149. A lot of work with professional people through the Center for Courage and Renewal (founded by Palmer) is "rejoining soul and role." Separation of soul and role occurs because sometimes we are in the right role but there is a disconnect with soul. Sometimes we are in the wrong role and the soul is trying to lead into a new role. "Role" is defined as the various roles we live: family, work, cultural, global, ethnic, and gender. These are the outside things that influence the inside of how we live our being. "Soul" is defined as the place where our truest self—the image of God unique for the individual—can dance and live with God's great delight.

hospitality and God's presence of love in ways that empower others. There are several spiritual practices that increase one's sense of power.

Making a power timeline, naming and noticing the times in life when he, she, or the congregation has felt powerful or powerless, is helpful. It is interesting that sometimes people do not like the word *power.* They have felt powerless so long that they do not yearn to claim their power. Incrementally over time, through spiritual direction, as the voice that has been silenced is regained, power is claimed.

Once one gains a sense of interior power, one seeks the other side of vulnerability. The other side of vulnerability is when a person can make his or her interior journey available for others. An available interior journey for others provides testimony to God's transfiguring love and grace. Individuals can look realistically at the world and at one's self while not getting stuck. This creates ministry and life vision by looking with the gaze of God's soft eyes upon the world and others. This type of vulnerability with the power of God is lived ethically as we see the Incarnation of Christ within others. This sense of power comes from the boldness of God's heart being formed deeply in the interior of self so that the individual can risk leading with courage, ethics, and live vision by trusting God in the midst of reality. It is here in claiming God's power within where authentic personal leadership is born.

More Than a Pipe Dream

It is more than a pipe dream, living from the four points of the Diamond Leadership Model—ethics, reality, vision, and power—merged with tools of spiritual direction training, to transfigure individuals and community into a new reality. As we are strengthened in our inner beings, becoming more Christlike in our worldview and love of self, others, and God, we have the personal power to look out for the best interest of others. It is this simultaneous increased personal leadership while descending the formational spiral that establishes a foundation for leadership in congregational ministry. These teachable tools are foundational to the soul of the congregation, not just a pipe dream.

Marjorie Thompson muses on what could happen if this was the inward posture within the church.

How much more precious [the church would be] if we really are willing to open our ears to the guidance of the spirit in real time. We don't have to be afraid of change and can hear clearly a word of guidance and know that we are moving in the direction that God has called us. . . . I am aware [that] some clergy and churches have begun doing this [leading from spiritual-direction-shaped formational core]. . . . Good leaders are careful to bring others on board so they experience the benefits of the practices. . . . I have observed this happening in a church in Denver. . . . It hasn't all been easy. People think it is silly not just to go by Robert's Rules and have a majority rule. But there are enough people there who are deeply committed to this because they have experienced the benefits firsthand . . . there is real potential for change.[10]

With Thompson's wider vision and hope for church transformation, it is clear how important education is for people to accept metamorphosis within the church. Thompson affirms weaving both informational academic work and formational experience for solid education and openness to God's formation. To move from pipe dreams to reality, we must ponder: How can we as leaders be transformed by the heartbeat of spiritual direction and formation? What is the cost to those outside the church who are searching for more than they have yet experienced? And the greatest question of all: What could be lost if this metamorphosis within the church does not transpire into reality?

Bearing the Fruits of Contemplation in the World

It is a small phrase, one that can easily get overlooked. "For the sake of the world" is how the classical definition of spiritual formation concludes. Spiritual direction is not just a feel-good experience for the believer. John Wesley tells us that the world is our parish. The deep-abiding question is, Can spiritual direction training make a difference in how church people not only relate to those within the church, but radiate God's love so others beyond the congregation also enter the metamorphic process?

The answer to this question is a resounding yes. While working secular jobs, the presence of God may be expressed and deepened, potentially

---

10 Buckwell, 166.

transfiguring workplace relationships and possibly the culture. Taking spiritual direction into the world may be as simple as learning to embrace people lightly. That is gazing upon them with God's soft eyes and seeing them as Christ. It may mean standing with those who are very different from self or from the church community and providing opportunity and space to hear and truly listen to their stories. This is the opportune time to build relationships beyond the church through holy listening. In the sixth section, we will join the monarch butterfly in freedom of flight. But before we move toward freedom of flight, please pause with the Spiritual Direction Readiness Assessment and Congregational Examen.

Spiritual Direction Readiness Assessment and Congregational Examen

At the end of each section is a Spiritual Direction Readiness Assessment and Congregational Examen. As mentioned earlier, consider creating a portfolio, either on the computer or with pencil and paper. Within this portfolio, record your responses to the assessment and examen. At the end of this book, review your portfolio of responses. Ponder how God is inviting you further into the metamorphosis process for leadership and within the church.

For this section, the Spiritual Direction Readiness Assessment and Congregational Examen will provide open opportunity to consider God's presence in and through personal and professional leadership. We joyfully discover that even now in the midst of our current realities, God shapes new life through struggle, questions, listening, prayer, and conversations. The wonder of examen is, What is the heartbeat of your leadership?

Worksheet of Examen: What Is the Heartbeat of Your Leadership?

Personal Leadership Assessment

A. Diamond Leadership Qualities
   a. What shape is your diamond?
   b. Which areas are strong, and which need attention?
   c. How do qualities of integrity, ethics, and power interface with the diamond points in your personal leadership?
   d. How does your personal leadership affect your professional leadership?
   e. What commitment and next step will you take for integrating tools from spiritual direction training into your leadership diamond?

B. Reality, Possibility, or Pipe Dream
   a. Who will work with and support your descending, metamorphic journey of transfiguration?
   b. What roadblocks rise before you?
   c. How will you celebrate God's presence in the midst of formation?

Please close your time of prayer with this or one of your own prayers.

I am humbled by your steadfast visionary presence, Lord. My heart joins with yours in hope and promise as your new possibilities are beginning to come out of the shadows of vague and misty vision. As you pour out your Holy Spirit upon me, may you open my heart to your greatest desire and possibility for me. I yearn to live as you love. Grant that my desires are not just pipe dreams, something that seems magical and unattainable. Fill my life with the breath of your Holy Spirit so that I may embody your new vision for leadership and ministry. Encourage my heart to obedience as I listen for the whispers of your direction. Thank you, Jesus, for becoming my spiritual director of personal life, vision, mission, and community. Amen.

Congregational Examen

A. Diamond Leadership Qualities
   a. What does the congregational diamond look like?
   b. Which areas are strong, and which need attention?
   c. How do qualities of integrity, ethics, and power interface with the diamond points in congregational personal leadership?
   d. How does parishioners' personal leadership affect congregational professional leadership?
   e. What commitment and next step will the congregation take for integrating tools from spiritual direction training into the congregational leadership diamond?
B. Reality, Possibility, or Pipe Dream
   a. Who are the Spirit-formed and Spirit-led leaders that will support and resource the congregation and individual parishioners as the church descends this metamorphic journey of transfiguration?
   b. What roadblocks rise before the congregation?
   c. How will the community celebrate God's presence in the midst of formation?

Interface of Personal and Congregational Responses

A. Are the leader and congregation in the same position of transfiguring metamorphosis?
B. What similarities between the leader and congregation do you notice?
C. What is different between the leader and congregation?
D. At what stage of awakening do you discern for yourself and for the congregation?
   a. *Disorientation:* How do you and the congregation experience chaos and confusion?
   b. *Heightened Search for God:* How have you and the congregation noticed an increased intentionality and search for the voice of truth, God's Divine presence in the midst of leadership, everyday life, and within the inner understanding of faith?
   c. *Change of Consciousness:* What new ways of prayer have taken hold within the congregation? Is the congregation ready to live from the

tools of spiritual direction? How is leadership and the congregation expanding new wings for flight?

E.   What is an invitation from God for moving forward *into* a transfiguring metamorphosis?

F.   What is the invitation from God for *descending* toward the heart of God into greater metamorphosis and awakening?

Please close your time of prayer with this or one of your own prayers.

> We are humbled by your steadfast visionary presence, Lord. Our hearts join with yours in hope and promise as your new possibilities are beginning to come out of the shadows of vague and misty vision. As you pour out your Holy Spirit upon this congregation, open our hearts to your greatest desire and possibility for us. We yearn to live as you love. Grant that our desires are not just pipe dreams, something that seems magical and unattainable. Fill our lives with the breath of your Holy Spirit so that we can come together embodying your new vision for leadership and ministry. Encourage our hearts to obedience as we listen together for the whispers of your direction. Thank you, Jesus, for becoming our spiritual director of congregational life, vision, mission, and community. Amen.

Six

SET FREE FOR FLIGHT

Beauty and joy shimmer as the authentic self ascends in flight. The monarch flies free. No longer constrained by the chrysalis, it is free to live as God's love intends. Whether it is a migrating generational butterfly or one that goes before the migration, the monarch is on its way. It only took a few hours to dry its wings after emerging easily from the chrysalis, and now it is set free. Its entire worldview has morphed from being earthbound. The monarch's ravenous hunger continues as it goes feasting on nectar from flower to flower so it can be sustained across the miles of its life pilgrimage.

Experiencing God's intimate love through the metamorphic process of transfiguration increases our hunger to rest, trust, and live in God. For us to be set free for flight, as Spirit-formed and Spirit-led leaders and congregations, the incandescent glow of God's love is illumined through our new ways of being in the world. Life is reoriented. New perspective is gained. Together we cocreate with God to move from the frenetic pace of the world. How will we, mere humans, sustain such lofty flight?

In this section, we take a long, loving look at what is most real. What we see with our physical eyes may not be what is most real. Together we explore contemporary ways to feast upon God, gaining inward sight and looking at the Incarnation of Christ among humanity. The Spiritual Direction

Readiness Assessment and Congregational Examen considers what internal and external influences urge us to God's new flight.

Like the migrating monarch, the church is built on generations before us. Each generation assists in coming to the opportune time of transfiguration. Similar to the migrating monarch, there are internal and external triggers for this generation to notice that now *is* the time of God's metamorphosis to new and deepened awakening.

The Generational Flight of the Monarch

Using their internal compass, monarchs traverse thousands of miles. They travel through good, sunny weather, seek shelter within trees, and find other way stations during the cool and stormy times. Remarkably, the migrating monarchs gain weight during their travel to Mexico. Their frequent feasting causes them to "store energy in the form of fat that will sustain them through the long winter."[1] Human beings can assist with the repopulation of the declining monarch species by providing way stations for rest along the migratory way. Kylee Baumle provides fantastic instruction on how to create a safe, sacred space for the migration of the monarchs.[2]

When the instinctive migratory pattern is expanded in consideration of the church, several questions cross my heart. Like the butterfly generations leading to the migratory generation, could God build up church generations leading to the metamorphic generation that sets the church into new flight? Are there internal yearnings that cause us to plumb the depths of Scripture, weave the cultural context through God's heart, and feel driven to articulate new ways of being church together? Could outside triggers like sexual abuse scandals, ethical decline, rigidity of extreme right or left political and theological positions, and waning participation signal our internal searching for the Divine? How does your heart burn with desire to notice God's power and presence even more profoundly, personally, and corporately through the shifting tides of culture?

---

1   Kylee Baumle. 2017. *The Monarch: Saving Our Most-Loved Butterfly.* Pittsburgh: St. Lynn's Press. Page 38.
2   Baumle, *The Monarch*, "Creating a Monarch Way Station," 105ff. The milkweed is most hospitable for raising four generations of monarch. She tells which trees, such as the willow, make ideal resting places during the long flight.

Taking a Long, Loving Look

The gift of spiritual direction trains the heart and mind to rest with contemplative pauses throughout the day. As one is formed by grace and strengthened to release more and more attachments, the pray-er gains freedom to truly claim his or her own belovedness. This gifts the pray-er with the wisdom to gaze upon others with compassion. This expands seeing God's beauty and presence beyond the beauty of sunrises, sunsets, and landscapes to see the indwelling of God in the eyes, actions, words, and mannerisms of other people. It is by taking this long, loving look at the other that we truly see the image of God within humanity.

God's long, loving gaze holds a different quality than looking at life or other people through the world's judgment of who is in and who is not. God's vision does not place judgment or look for ways to entrap us. In our communal silence, God resides between us as well as within us. Taking a long, loving look assists us in remaining silent. Being gazed upon by another through the lens of God-love creates our communities differently as we are more fully living Christlikeness.

God loves. Those trained with tools from spiritual direction see and hear the Incarnation of God's love within the other. We are the beloved ones of God. The more comfortable we become receiving God's tender gaze of love, the wider our loving gaze can look upon others and self without judgment. Through the use of spiritual direction tools, our worldview shifts to one full of compassion. This becomes a huge cultural shift. The imperfections and differences of the other fall away as the *Imago Dei* ("image of God") becomes most prominent to the Spirit-formed and Spirit-led person's view.

As we turn our long, loving gaze toward the contemporary church with the tools of spiritual direction, truly we celebrate the opportunity of moving through the chaos toward a new change of consciousness for viewing God's beautiful beloved church.

From Frenetic Action to Daily Practice

I have intentionally taken years to grow in my own understanding and experience for the writing of this book. This varied, expansive foundation confirms for me the time *is* now. God is opening the way through the frenetic days of our current culture for expanded formational practices personally and in community. A contemplative way of life born from spiritual direction training does lead to new possibility.

A Contemplative Way

We do not have God all figured out. God is always a creative and creating God. God desires to communicate with us individually and as community. Why do we become fearful, competitive, or threatened when the depth of yearning is met with new response? Is not our truest hope and security in God? Have we ever come to a point when the theological argument of what we have deemed to be right and wrong becomes seemingly more important than even our love for Jesus?

The way of contemplation leads us beyond these surface and emotionally charged issues in a descent toward the heart of God. As we have noted through testimonies, the contemplative way of seeing and hearing others gifts us with new lenses through which to view not only the world, but our communities and personal relationships. With greater knowledge of our personal story as attachments are released, healed, and loved into new beauty, we are able to hold others lightly without judgment, coercion, or the need to set others straight. From this stable foundation in our belovedness, individuals and congregations are even better able to enter into silence. Through this contemplative stance in relationship with God and expansive comfort with silence, the way opens so that we do not need to power up or strive for affirmation from others. Our trust foundation of God and in God becomes all encompassing. This affects every arena of our lives and ministry.

When teaching the heartbeat of leadership, I have a slide that depicts the Olympic rings. These slightly overlapping circles represent, for me, all arenas of life. These could be finances, relationships, health, spiritual formation, silence, education, work, Sabbath, recreation, and much more. The contemplative life gives harmony to all arenas of our lives individually and within community. I intentionally use the word *harmony* rather than *balance*. Imbalances may crop up. Things like illness may strike, making finances tighter than normal. Or working in the church, the liturgical seasons may affect hours spent at work, or funerals may need to be officiated. However, the practitioner of spiritual direction always seeks harmony among all these arenas of life. If for a time greater attention is needed in one arena, the

Spirit-formed and Spirit-led persons intentionally shift focus by highlighting the other arenas for a time. This creates harmony for life.

As we move from the frenetic way of life to this contemplative harmony with God, it is imperative to remember two very important words: *detachment* and *attachment*. Think about the intentional contemplation from John 21, as the resurrected Jesus asks Peter, "Do you love me more than these?" What are your "these"? What emotions, things, people, places, thoughts, theological positions, habits, and hang-ups do you individually and collectively need to detach from to be more nearly conformed inwardly to God's formative love this day?

Through this intention of detaching our "more than these," we are given an even greater attachment to love of God. Our stability in heart and faith expands so that we are not thrown off on tangents of worry or pummeled with seemingly insurmountable problems. Yes, we still get angry. Yes, we still get afraid, feel bits of jealousy, or perceive to be threatened by the good fortune of others. But now we will have new tools for coping. We intentionally choose how we will react. As the *pneuma*, the very breath of God, fills our being, individually and collectively we live into a change of consciousness. As we proceed through the process of metamorphosis we are no longer trapped in our stuckness. It is here as our inward holiness of attachment to Jesus increases in the depth of our being that we are transfigured through consistent practice of spiritual direction training tools within interpersonal and public relationships. Beyond the tools of spiritual direction training already mentioned, here are a few fun ways to increase inward holiness among community.

Contemporary Prayer Practices

Prayer is much more than evoking the name of God for fulfillment of our hopes, dreams, and desires or to transform, create, and redeem the object of our prayer. Prayer transfigures the heart of us pray-ers as we become even more willing to lay aside our agendas. Ancient ways of opening to God have been mentioned previously. *Lectio Divina* may be prayed through other senses such as sight and hearing. These forms of prayer are called *Visio Divina* and *Audio Divina*.

Visio *and* Audio Divina

Divine seeing, *Visio Divina*, is a prayer experience that all ages can enjoy. *Visio Divina* encompasses ancient prayer disciplines such as icon gazing, the creation and viewing of stained-glass windows, participating in stations of the cross, and looking upon natural land and urban scenes. It can also encompass the way that we look upon other people, if we are willing to look beyond the surface to the Incarnation of Christ. "An important dynamic of *Visio Divina* is to expect to encounter the living Word of God through the ordinary means of technology. God's Word is whispered to us through human voice, song, scripture, silence, picture, images, and many other ways. We are not making the image into God but using the video image as a vehicle to hear God's voice."[3]

One of my favorite practices of *Visio Divina* is with movies.

If the video is a major motion picture or lengthy in duration, please choose a short two- to three-minute segment of the video. If you do not have computer access, there is no problem. Do you watch television or live streaming? Do you have a DVD or Blu-Ray player? Any video or television show can be viewed and prayed with *Visio Divina*. Television shows are a little more difficult unless you can pause and rewind the show easily. Some may even want to watch a portion of a show on the small screen of their smartphone![4]

After you have viewed your video clip, you are ready to pray. If you are watching the video clip on your computer, please cover the computer screen between viewings so that you will not be distracted. This prayer discipline follows a similar format to *Lectio Divina*. You will watch the video clip three or four times depending on how familiar you are with the show. After each viewing, give yourself or the community plenty of time for contemplative silence as you consider how God may be whispering to your heart.

1. On the first viewing, notice what segment of the video catches your attention. What stands out to your mind and heart as you watch the video segment? After watching the clip and having silent reflection time, share with your community what stood out most for you during this viewing. Simply naming the portion of the scene without explanation is helpful.

2. On the second viewing, notice how the video segment intersects your life or the ministry of your community. After the silent

---

3   Brenda Buckwell. 2016. *The Advent of God's Word: Listening for the Power of the Divine Whisper.* Woodstock, VT: Skylight Paths Publishing. 46.

4   Buckwell, *The Advent of God's Word,* 47.

reflection time, share your responses of connection with the video clip. This is likely to be longer than a one-word response.

3. On the third viewing, notice what invitation from God you notice for self or community. It could be an invitation to be something or do something—possibly an invitation to trust, have courage, or to act concretely in the way you express God's love to others. If you are praying together in community, the leader may want to write down the invitations shared around the group. After the sharing is complete is the final step of blessing.

4. If you are praying *Visio Divina* in a group setting, this fourth step is vitally important in that it opens the way for prayer. Each person will pray for the individual on his or her right. This is not just any prayer; rather, the pray-er prays for the invitation that the person heard to become reality in his or her life, moving the pray-er from an individual perspective to being knit together deeper in the heart of God's prayer.

Audio Divina, or divine listening, may be practiced as illustrated above; however, instead of a video segment, music is the key. Listening to music is a joy to the soul. You can download selections of music for prayer-filled enjoyment, listen to live musicians, or even listen closely to the aliveness of nature. As you listen, pray through the steps above as you deepen your contemplative way of life.

Photo Pilgrimage

Another fun prayer discipline is taking contemplative pictures. There is a gift in slowing down to take a picture. The photographer watches for little nudges from and listens for whispers of God. What is God inviting you to take a picture of? Once the pictures are taken, they may be viewed for prayer with *Visio Divina*. All pictures have the potential for prayer. From the beautiful vistas of the countryside to the urban sprawl of the city, God's presence and Word may illumine your picture-taking walk.

Taking a long, loving look at people, places, and things provides an opportunity to imagine how God sees beyond the surface presentation of our lives, human events, and relationships. This contemplative gaze unstops our hearing so that we can listen with our whole being to notice what our soul is attracted to. Then, the prayerful pilgrim gains freedom to look for new and diverse perspectives, notice light and shadows, and focus on the object of the soul's desire.

In preparation for a photo pilgrimage, you will need a camera for taking pictures. This can be a smartphone or a complex camera with various shutter speeds and lenses to focus. When considering what picture to take, contemplate the angles of light, the shadows, the brightness, and the allure of the object to your spirit.

The process for this prayer discipline is a simple one.

Center: What most invites you into awareness of God's presence—mantra, silence, breath prayer? Then once you discern the direction and location of your walk, begin asking God to draw you to see what God desires you to notice.

Stop, look, and listen: As you wander along, pause when you feel prompted by God's inward nudge. Look around and see what your attention settles on. Listen for the voice of God whispering to you, inviting you to gaze closely upon an object.

Gaze upon the object in prayer: Once you have been drawn by God to an object, scene in nature, person, or place, begin praying while you take your photographs. Your prayer may be a wonder about how God is present and whispering to you from this object.

Focus: While you are praying and slowly taking pictures from various angles, heights, and distances, notice the different focus of lens needed for each shot. Even smartphones have zoom features to make your pictures distinctive.

Change perspective: While you are praying and slowly taking pictures, consider the perspective from which you are looking. You may desire to try a picture from above the object, straight on, or from below. Each new perspective or angle causes the selected object to glisten just a bit differently.

Attend to light and shadows: While you are praying and slowly taking pictures, consider the way the light and shadows dance around, across, and through the illumination of your object. Each item being photographed is a creation of God. From steel-manufactured beams to a single blade of grass peeking through the hardened earth, God's creative Word is present.

Notice how the differing perspective, light, and focus bring different insights. These insights may intensify even after the fact of picture taking when you spend contemplative time praying with *Visio Divina* through your photographs.

When you have finished your contemplative walk, give thanks to God for the prayer-filled insights from the object of your contemplative photography.

These three contemporary prayer tools, *Visio Divina*, *Audio Divina*, and contemplative photography, are fun ways to engage people of all ages and stages of faith in contemplation. They lead to taking a long, loving look at what is truly real—that is, seeing God's presence within. As we practice these and other spiritual tools, we are set free for flight in love of God, others, and self.

Spiritual Direction Readiness Assessment and Congregational Examen

At the end of each section is a Spiritual Direction Readiness Assessment and Congregational Examen. As mentioned earlier, consider creating a portfolio, either on the computer or with pencil and paper. Within this portfolio, record your responses to the assessment and examen. At the end of this book, review your portfolio of responses. Ponder how God is inviting you further into the metamorphosis process for leadership and within the church.

The Spiritual Direction Readiness Assessment and Congregational Examen will provide questions pondering the practices of this section and the possibility of being set free for flight. Standing upon the foundation of church generations before us, we move from frenetic action to a daily practice of grounding, centering, and opening a congregation and the leadership through tools of spiritual direction training. The question of where and how to begin is relevant. As the generation for metamorphosis and awakening in the church, what will be the congregation's next step? The questions of this examen are: How do you take a long, loving look at self, others, and God, and what are the implications of this gaze?

WORKSHEET OF EXAMEN: HOW DO YOU TAKE A LONG, LOVING LOOK AT SELF, OTHERS, AND GOD?

Personal Leadership Assessment

A. The Practice of Spiritual Disciplines
    a. How many times a week and for how long do you practice silence?
    b. What is your favorite spiritual discipline to routinely and regularly practice? What kind of rhythm do you create for yourself?
    c. How do you pray the Scriptures as well as study them?
    d. Which contemporary practice will you begin incorporating into your daily disciplines?
    e. What next step will you take to expand creativity and compassion through your spiritual disciplines?
B. A Long, Loving Look
    a. How comfortable are you gazing closely at your interior life and another's?
    b. What is that like for you?
    c. What skills does it take to release all evaluative thoughts and simply receive the other?
    d. How comfortable are you at having another gaze lovingly upon your interior heart? What could increase your comfort level?

Please close your time of prayer with this or one of your own prayers.

Holy and Gracious God, open my heart that I may hear the still, small voice within your whispering silence. Open the way for your inner voice of wisdom within silence to guide my thoughts, actions, and words throughout my days. Gift me with an assurance of your presence so that I may bask in your Divine gaze of love, even when that comes from other people. I trust you and seek to experience the depths of your transfiguring love. May my life become so luminous with your presence that when people look upon me they see your loving presence. Amen.

Congregational Examen

A. Practice of Spiritual Disciplines
    a. How many times a week and for how long does the congregation practice silence?
    b. What is the congregation's favorite spiritual discipline to routinely and regularly practice? What is the regular rhythm of practices for the congregation?
    c. How does the congregation pray the Scriptures as well as study them?
    d. Which contemporary practice will the congregation begin incorporating into weekly disciplines?
    e. What next step will the congregation take to expand creativity and compassion through spiritual disciplines?
B. A Long, Loving Look
    a. How comfortable is the congregation with the practice of someone gazing with great love at them?
    b. How does the congregation gaze upon others?
    c. How do we encourage others to feel very comfortable receiving the loving gaze of others?

Interface of Personal and Congregational Responses

A. Are the leader and congregation in the same position of transfiguring metamorphosis?
B. What similarities between the leader and congregation do you notice?
C. What is different between the leader and congregation?
D. At what stage of awakening do you discern for yourself and for the congregation?
    a. *Disorientation:* How do you and the congregation experience chaos and confusion?
    b. *Heightened Search for God:* How have you and the congregation noticed an increased intentionality and search for the voice of truth, God's Divine presence in the midst of leadership, everyday life, and within the inner understanding of faith?
    c. *Change of Consciousness:* What new ways of prayer have taken hold within the congregation? Is the congregation ready to live new

things? How is leadership and the congregation expanding new wings for flight?

E. What is an invitation from God for moving forward *into* a transfiguring metamorphosis?

F. What is the invitation from God for *descending* toward the heart of God into greater metamorphosis and awakening?

Please close your time of prayer with this or one of your own prayers.

Holy and Gracious God, open our hearts so that we may hear the still, small voice within your whispering silence. Open the way for your inner voice of wisdom within silence to guide our thoughts, actions, and words as a congregation throughout the days. Gift us with an assurance of your presence so that we may bask in your Divine gaze of love, even when that comes from other people. We trust you and seek to experience the depths of your transfiguring love. May this church become so luminous with your presence that when people look upon us they see your loving presence. Amen.

Afterword

Awakening to a New Reality

The monarch flies. This pollinator cocreates with God life beyond itself. There is no going back to the old ways of living. The butterfly spreads its wings and takes flight as God's transfigured creation. The Methuselah generation becomes the hope of today and for tomorrow.

Could it be that the church has been inadvertently seeking shelter in our cultural storm of disorientation? Have church people turned inward, gathered together like those under an umbrella seeking safety from the cultural chaos? Has the church shied away from the risk of being boldly countercultural? Has it become time for a Methuselah generation to rise up within the church? The image of the church becoming a way station, nourishing the depths of the soul, ignites my heart with hope.

This afterword offers imaginative thoughts and practical suggestions for implementing spiritual direction and the tools from spiritual direction training into the congregation. This section concludes with a final portion for leaders, pastors, teachers, and staff, providing resources for implementation for spiritual direction training to catalyze the metamorphic transfiguration of church.

Taking Flight

When the day of Pentecost came, they were all together in one place. Suddenly a sound like the blowing of a violent wind came from heaven and filled the whole house. . . . Then Peter stood up with the Eleven, raised his voice and addressed the crowd: . . . "God says, I will pour out my Spirit on all people. Your sons and daughters will prophesy, your young men will see visions, your old men will dream dreams." (Acts 2:1–2, 14, 17b, NIV)

161

Pentecost living continues today as God's dreams are dreamed and people imagine new ways of living in community as faithful believers in Jesus. Having made huge transitions because of the pandemic and civil protest, we are now living on the verge of a new awakening. Is the rejoining of the mystical and academic disciplines of faith possible? Yes.

Tilden Edwards reminds us that there is a "need to account for differing levels of experience that people bring—that means it can't be a cookie cutter kind of formation. . . . The question of [the] voluntary nature of training, I find important. When you are dealing with the clergyperson's spiritual life—it is so intrusive to require it."[1]

What would happen if mainline connectional churches such as the Methodists, Lutherans, Presbyterians, Baptists, Episcopalians, and United Church of Christ offered spiritual direction training as part of the ordination process? What could it look like for ecumenical or denominational geographic areas to create a rhythm of spiritual direction and training in preparation for ordination? Could this training be designed as a hybrid of face-to-face and online video conferences or totally online? Again, yes.

Here is one proposal for implementing a three-year experience of spiritual direction training in judicatories for those in the process of ordination or during the seminary journey.

Year One

The topic for the first year is individual spiritual direction, and the focus is on building spiritual muscle and increasing stability.

Year Two

The topic for year two is group spiritual direction, and the focus is triad learning and practice within group spiritual direction with real plays of director, directee, and observer. Additional foci include formation questions, levels of storytelling and listening, counter-story, and the importance of knowing one's self with the study of St. Teresa of Ávila and St. John of the Cross.

Year Three

The teaching topic for year three is corporate spiritual direction. The focus is on integrating tools of spiritual direction training as foundation for the soul of the congregation.

---

1   Buckwell, *Resdicovering the Contemplative Tradition*, 170.

Year Four

The topic of this optional year is spiritual direction into community beyond the congregation, and the focus is on mission. This will highlight the final clause of the definition of spiritual formation, "for the sake of others"; that is, mission born through Christlikeness. With neighborhoods and nations as a laboratory, participants learn how to use the tools of spiritual direction training in outreach ministry, training laity to use spiritual direction in the workplace and how spiritual direction offers the Third Way of nonviolence in transforming the world.

These educational events also prepare congregations for receiving pastors trained in spiritual direction since parishioners are invited to attend in part the residential retreats yearly.

What about Seminaries?

What could be the ramifications if seminaries considered expanding the formational programs and spiritual direction stance within academia? Is there a way to rejoin the longstanding Western split between theological information and the mystic experience in education? Could contextual individual, group, and corporate spiritual direction influence how and what is taught in seminaries? The final two-pronged query related to seminaries as people are formed for ministerial leadership through an educational process is, How could training in spiritual direction assist the endorsing agencies and boards of ordained ministry?

Living from a New Perspective

Parishioners and leaders live from a new perspective as tools of spiritual direction training become foundational within the congregation, education, and the ordination and endorsing process. There are several creative ways to address the issue of taking spiritual direction into the community beyond the congregation. One may want to role-play working as a lawyer (or any given profession) to discover ways to converse with a spiritual direction basis with one's clients or colleague. What about conversations at the coffee shop? Or inviting people into community ministry; taking intentional time to listen to his or her stories of hardship; and offering opportunity for noticing God even in the midst of poverty, prejudice, and injustices of the world? When spiritual direction is taken into the community beyond the church, the culture at large potentially awakens to a new mode of being.

The tools of spiritual direction training and an expanded perspective of spiritual direction beyond the religious community into the secular world could have enormous ramifications. The hunger is present and rampant. Yet it is not my hunger alone. The world is waiting. Now is the time for the church to rise from the disorientation and chaos of the world and take flight as new creations in Christ shining as a light to the nations.

Resources

Living Streams Flowing Water offers resources for teachers, pastors, judicatory personnel, and lay leadership. When you go to the website www.living streamsflowingwater.com you will find an interactive section for readers and resources from me, Brenda, awaiting you. These include but are not limited to

- a personal greeting from me;
- an instructional PowerPoint for leading congregational teams through this book; and/or
- spiritual coaching or supervision conversation.

For individual or group spiritual direction, or to invite me to consult with your congregation, judicatory, or national event, please contact me through the website. I am happy to assist you with all your spiritual formation consultative needs.

Training Resources for Spiritual Direction

- CenterQuest is an ecumenical hub for the study and practice of Christian spirituality: www.cqcenterquest.org.
- The Rueben P. Job Institute for Spiritual Formation: www.garrett.edu /centers-and-institutes/rueben-p-job-institute-spiritual-formation.
- Living Streams Flowing Water, A Spiritual Formation Ministry Online: www.livingstreamsflowingwater.com.
- Center for Action and Contemplation: www.cac.org.
- Renovare Institute for Christian Spiritual Formation: www.Renovare .org.
- Shalem Institute for Spiritual Formation: www.shalem.org.
- Mercy Center: Conferences, Retreat, and Spiritual Programing: www.mercy-center.org.

- Spiritual Directors International, The Home of Spiritual Companion-ship: www.sdiworld.org.

Bibliography for Spiritual Direction and Training Tools of Spiritual Direction

Artress, Lauren. 1995. *Walking a Sacred Path.* New York: The Berkley Publishing Group.

Benner, David G. 2010. *Opening to God: Lectio Divina and Life as Prayer.* Downers Grove, IL: InterVarsity Press.

Blythe, Teresa A. 2006. *50 Ways to Pray: Practices from Many Traditions and Times.* Nashville, TN: Abingdon Press.

Blythe, Teresa A., and Daniel Wolpert. 2004. *Meeting God in Virtual Reality: Using Spiritual Practices with Media.* Convergence Series. Nashville, TN: Abingdon Press.

Boa, Ken. 2001. *Conformed to His Image: Biblical and Practical Approaches to Spiritual Formation.* Grand Rapids, MI: Zondervan Publishing House.

Bondi, Roberta C. 1998. *A Place to Pray: Reflections on the Lord's Prayer.* Nashville, TN: Abingdon Press.

Buckwell, Brenda K. 2016. *The Advent of God's Word: Listening for the Power of the Divine Whisper.* Woodstock, VT: Skylight Paths Publishing.

———. 2007. *Rediscovering the Contemplative Tradition: The Formation of Protestant Clergy as Spiritual Directors within the Twenty-First Century.* A field research project report in partial fulfillment of requirements for the degree of doctor of ministry. Garrett-Evangelical Theological Seminary, Evanston, IL.

Chambers, Oswald. 1993. *Prayer: A Holy Occupation.* Grand Rapids, MI: Discovery House Publishers.

Forest, Jim. 2006. *Praying with Icons.* New York: Orbis Books.

Forman, Mary. 2005. *Praying with the Desert Mothers.* Collegeville, MN: Liturgical Press.

Foster, Richard, J. 1981. *Freedom of Simplicity.* San Francisco: HarperSanFrancisco.

Foster, Richard J., and Emilie Griffin. 2000. *Spiritual Classics: Selected Readings for Individual Groups on the Twelve Spiritual Disciplines.* San Francisco: HarperSan Francisco.

Fryling, Alice. 2003. *The Art of Spiritual Listening: Responding to God's Voice Amid the Noise of Life.* New York: WaterBrook Press.

Hall, Sister Jeremy. 2007. *Silence, Solitude, Simplicity: A Hermit's Love Affair with a Noisy, Crowded and Complicated World.* Collegeville, MN: Liturgical Press.

Keating, Thomas. 1994. *Intimacy with God.* New York: Crossroad Publishing.

Kincannon, Karla M. 2005. *Creativity and Divine Surprise.* Nashville, TN: Upper Room Books.

Laird, Martin. 2006. *Into the Silent Land: A Guide to Christian Contemplation.* New York: Oxford University Press.

Lindahl, Kay. 2002. *The Sacred Art of Listening: Forty Reflections for Cultivating a Spiritual Practice.* Woodstock, VT: Skylight Paths Publishing.

————. 2003. *Practicing the Sacred Art of Listening: A Guide to Enrich Your Relationships and Kindle Your Spiritual Life.* Woodstock, VT: Skylight Paths Publishing.

Maas, Robin, and Gabriel O'Donnell, editors. 1990. *Spiritual Traditions for the Contemporary Church.* Nashville, TN: Abingdon Press.

MacBeth, Sybil. 2007. *Praying in Color: Drawing a New Path to God.* Brewster, MA: Paraclete Press.

Merton, Thomas. 1971. *Contemplative Prayer.* Garden City, NY: Doubleday.

Mullholland, Robert. 1985. *Shaped by the Word: The Power of Scripture in Spiritual Formation.* Nashville, TN: Upper Room Books.

————. 1993. *Invitation to a Journey: A Road Map for Spiritual Formation.* Downers Grove, IL: InterVarsity Press.

Nouwen, Henri. 1991. *Thomas Merton: Contemplative Critic.* New York: Triumph Books.

————. 1997. *Bread for the Journey: A Daybook of Wisdom and Faith.* San Francisco: HarperSanFrancisco.

————. 1997. *Living in the Presence of God: The Everyday Spirituality of Brother Lawrence.* South Bend, IN: Ave Maria Press.

————. 1999. *The Only Necessary Thing: Living a Prayerful Life,* edited by W. Greer. New York: Crossroad Publishing.

Steere, Douglas. 2002. *Dimensions of Prayer: Cultivating a Relationship with God.* Nashville, TN: Upper Room Books.

Teresa of Ávila. 1989. *The Interior Castle,* translated by E. Allison Peers. New York: Image Books.

Willard, Dallas. 1988. *The Spirit of the Disciplines: Understanding How God Changes Lives.* New York: HarperCollins.

APPENDIX A

A CONTEMPORARY RULE OF LIFE
FOR SPIRITUAL DIRECTION

This appendix is designed to create a Rule of Life with the tools from spiritual direction training.[1] First consider this: What do you drop from your schedule when your time becomes very committed? Do you tend to lose prayer time, time of personal exercise, family time, or playtime? As way of final Spiritual Direction Readiness Assessment, this Rule of Life is directed toward discerning what steps you will commit to for utilizing tools of spiritual direction training.

- What tools from spiritual direction training am I attracted to and why?
- Where do I feel God is calling me to stretch and grow?
- What tools could give balance to my life?
  - _____ I will seek out/continue a relationship with a spiritual director.
  - _____ I will seek out/continue a relationship with a pastoral counselor.
  - _____ I will seek out/continue an accountability relationship with _____. (examples: coach, covenant group, a spiritual direction training program)

In the area of Know Thyself, I will do the following.

- In my personal leadership, a personal discipline I intend to practice is _____.
- To become a non-anxious presence within my life, I will _____.
- In concern for the world, I will pray for _____.
- In response to my concern for the world, I will practice holy listening and storytelling, as I serve through _____.
- In response to my concern for the world, I will practice formational questions, through _____.

---

1   This is modeled after Dr. Dwight Judy, handout from the Doctor of Ministry class at Garrett-Evangelical Theological Seminary.

I will serve God by doing the following.

- In my family, I will _____.
- In my neighborhood, I will _____.
- To the nations, I will _____.

To care for my physical body, I will do the following.

- Practice deep listening with the discipline of silence regularly: *(name duration of time and number of days per week)*
- In the arena of nutrition, I will _____.
- In the venue of exercise, I will _____.

A personal issue/attitude I will observe is _____.

To pay attention to these areas of potential development, I will review them regularly, making journal notes of my relationship to the issue. If possible I will share my progress at monthly gatherings with a spiritual director or in group spiritual direction.

_____

Signed   Date

For a period from _____ until _____

APPENDIX B

DAILY EXAMEN

The intent of examen is to consciously notice how God was present and active during daily life. I liken Daily Examen to an archeologist. Just as the archeologist intentionally excavates the earth for hidden treasure, so the spiritual seeker excavates the heart and soul for the hidden treasures of God's whispering presence.[2]

Daily Examen is a way of listening beyond the surface of events, conversations, and daily happenings. As you review the past twenty-four hours, morning, afternoon, or week, your inner eye of the heart and the wisdom of God will assist you in searching out the hidden treasures of God.

_____

2   Brenda Buckwell. 2015. *The Advent of God's Word: Listening for the Divine Whisper.* Woodstock, VT: Skylight Paths Publishing. Page 130.

Begin by looking in the rearview mirror at your day's events. "Gaze upon them with the eyes and heart of God. Remember gazing with God's soft eyes is letting go of judgmental, critical, and analytical thoughts and seeing beyond the surface to the interior heart of your creation.... Ponder the examen questions":[3]

- How do I see God's consolation through this time period (God's presence and activity)?
- How do I notice God's desolation through this time period (God's absence and mystery)?
- What will I do differently tomorrow to notice even more of God's activity in my life?

This can be done in community or personally. In community, people have the opportunity to engage in the discovery of how God is present and unnoticeable to our lives.

APPENDIX C
MOVIE MEDITATION, BREATH PRAYER AND WALKING MEDITATION, PRAYING WITH ICONS

"Learn to see God in the details of your life, for [God] is everywhere."

—Teresa of Ávila, fifteenth-century mystic

Movie Meditation (*Visio Divina*)

This sample of movie meditation is from the motion picture *It's a Wonderful Life*. Three scenes are selected for your meditative viewing, rather than viewing the same video segment three times. These scenes depict a possible progression of spirituality and mental health. Each person, at some time or another throughout his or her life, goes through stages of searching beyond self for relief and healing. As you view the scene, please respond to the formational questions.

3   Buckwell, *Advent of God's Word*, 131.

1. Scene 21: Start at 1:38:29, and end after the line "That is what I get for praying."
   — *Reflection Question:* What word or phrase from this clip catches your attention?
   — *The Spiritual Journey:* When life is difficult, people often find the strength to reach out beyond self.
2. Scene 22: Start at 2:012, and end after the line "I jumped in to save you."
   — *Reflection Question:* Where does this intersect with your life or the life of one you know?
   — *The Spiritual Journey:* Companions are needed for healing.
3. Scene 26: Start at 20:1:26, and end after the line "A toast to the richest man in town."
   — *Reflection Questions:* Who encourages you or someone you know to live a transfigured and healed life? With whom will you share the strength and conviction of your new life?
   — *The Spiritual Journey:* Sometimes we do not realize when new life is starting to happen. Others may notice first. Transformation, even though no circumstances have changed, is an internal attitudinal change. Reentry into community in a new way, with a new perspective and renewed love, is possible.

The use of movies on the journey of faith or the healing journey can expand imagination, open possibilities, bolster courage, and create role models.

Breath Prayer with Walking Meditation

The breath prayer lies within us like a tiny seed that, when nurtured, flowers into a new and deeper awareness of God's presence. To discover your breath prayer, follow these five easy steps. Once your breath prayer is discovered, you may use it with walking meditation.

For walking meditation, please inhale the phrase of your prayer while you are slowly taking a step forward. Exhale all resistance to the prayer on the next step. Repeat with each step.

The name of this prayer comes from the Hebrew word *ruach* and Greek word *pneuma*, meaning Spirit, breath, or wind of God. Breathe in slowly through the nose and exhale through slightly parted lips. Generally, this rhythm of breathing synchs nicely with a phrase of about six to eight syllables. Here are a few examples of breath prayers.

Lord, open the way.
Jesus, grant me peace.
Enfold me, God, in your love.
Let me know your comfort, Father.

Breath prayers are formed by contemplating your heart's greatest desire, which is formed into a six- to eight-syllable phrase. This is then yoked with your favorite name for God. Discerning God's wisdom takes time. First thoughts that often jump to mind are for immediate hopes, needs, and wants. Here are some examples of first thoughts or concerns that may come to mind.

Protect my friend's unborn child.
Give Aunt Suzie rest and healing.
Help me to find a job, home, friends, or _____.
Forgive me for _____.
Open the way for reconciliation with _____.

These immediate prayers are vital and important prayers. But a breath prayer even goes deeper to your heart's desire than situational prayers. To understand further the depth of a breath prayer, look at your hand. The palm of your hand is surrounded by fingers and thumb. The breath prayer is like the palm of your hand; it supports and brings life and vitality to the fingers (specific situational prayers). An illustration of a breath prayer: "Jesus, let me live as you love." The more one learns to live as Jesus' loves, the more this prayer supports and encourages daily life.

To discover your heart's deepest desire during your breath prayer, keep in mind the following.

1. Center yourself into quiet prayer.
2. Once your heart is quiet and you are open to hearing God-wisdom, imagine Jesus sitting right in front of you.
3. While Jesus is listening both intently and lovingly *and* gazing upon you, imagine him asking you: "*Name,* what would you like me to do for you?" Spend significant time in contemplative, quiet prayer with this question.

4. Once you have a broad answer to the above question, write that phrase. Narrow it to six to eight syllables.
5. Consider your favorite or most used name for God. These might include Lord, Jesus, God, Great Spirit, Creator.
6. Put it all together, with your favorite name for God either at the beginning or end of your six- to eight-syllable phrase.

You may find that once you have prayed with your newly created breath prayer, a word needs to be switched, or the name for God feels like it should change. This is how God assists in fine-tuning your breath prayer to shape you into praying exactly the best breath prayer for you.[4]

Walking meditation with breath prayer simply combines the two techniques. Walking meditation is intentionally slowing the pace of steps down to match the rate of your breathing with the breath prayer. This truly slows the speed of walking down. In fact, you may notice you are a bit wobbly walking that slowly. Balance will be regained as you descend nearer the heart of God through this walking meditation.

Praying with Icons

Icons are windows to God. They are to be read like the Word of God, not just looked at on the surface. Icon gazing—that is, gazing with the long, loving look of God—is a historic way of listening with our entire body and seeing beyond the surface of presented events, words, and relationships.

The process for the creation of an icon by iconographer follows.

*   Creating an icon is a work of prayer.
*   Icons are written with prayer and fasting.
*   To become an iconographer, one is blessed and commissioned for this work.
*   The iconographer prays a twofold prayer with each stroke of the brush:
    — For the icon, that it be infused with the creative presence of God.
    — For the one who looks upon the icon, that he or she may experience the living presence of God.

---

4   Ron DelBene with Herb Montgomery. 1983. *The Hunger of the Heart.* San Francisco: Harper & Row. Modified by Buckwell.

- There is always a space within the icon that invites the one gazing upon it to be invited into God's presence.
- The iconographer sees him- or herself as a co-creator with God in humility and thanksgiving.
- To pray with icons, consider the following practices.
- Praying with icons often occurs in candlelight.
- Pray expectantly, looking and listening.
- If we do not see God in the created order around us, we will never see God in the face of the other.[5]

---

5   This section is informed by Jim Forest. 2006. *Praying with Icons*. New York: Orbis Books.

CPSIA information can be obtained
at www.ICGtesting.com
Printed in the USA
LVHW111138060822
725316LV00001B/207